THE INDIANAPOLIS STAR

Jeff Gordon
BURNING UP THE TRACK

SP
SPORTS
PUBLISHING
L.L.C.

Acknowledgments

When Jeff Gordon strapped in for his first race at Atlanta Motor Speedway in November 1992, no one had any idea what this young phenom would accomplish in the next 10 years. Since then he has gone on to win four Winston Cup titles and is the only NASCAR driver to win three times at the famed Indianapolis Motor Speedway. He has gone from rookie driver to Winston Cup champion to car owner and mentor for the up-and-coming Jimmie Johnson. What he chooses to accomplish next seems to be only whatever he makes his mind up to do. *The Indianapolis Star* has covered Jeff Gordon since his sprint car days and has documented his climb to success and subsequent stardom in one of the most competitive and rapidly growing sports in America.

Bringing this story to life each day in the pages of *The Indianapolis Star* took the hard work and dedication of many people at the paper. We especially wish to thank Barbara A. Henry (President and Publisher), Terry Eberle (Editor and Vice President), Tim Wheatley (Assistant Managing Editor/Sports), Jim Lefko (Sports Editor), Charlie Nye (Assistant Managing Editor/Photography), Mike Fender (Director of Photography), Michael Jesse (Library Director) and Cathy Knapp (Assistant Library Director). Without their assistance and efficiency this project would not have gotten off the ground.

Space limitations preclude us from thanking all the writers and photographers whose contributions appear in this book. However, where available, we have preserved the writers' bylines and the photographers' credits to ensure proper attribution for their work.

To Mark Garrow, who once again has provided us with the most comprehensive and compelling audio for the CD, we appreciate all of your hard work and dedication.

Lastly, I am thankful for all of the support and effort of those at Sports Publishing who have been nothing short of enthusiastic toward this project: to Peter Bannon and Joe Bannon, Jr. for giving me the opportunity to have the career of a lifetime, to Susan Moyer for her vast knowledge and friendship, to Jeff Higgerson for giving me guidance and direction, to Erin Linden-Levy, who is simply a wealth of information, and to Cindy McNew for ensuring that what we put out is fully edited and fact-checked. Thanks also to Roger Dale Coad for his inspirational design efforts.

Lynnette A. Bogard
Coordinating Editor

Jeff Gordon
BURNING UP THE TRACK

Publisher: **Peter L. Bannon**

Senior Managing Editor: **Joseph J. Bannon, Jr.**

Coordinating Editor: **Lynnette A. Bogard**

Art Director: **K. Jeffrey Higgerson**

Graphic Designer: **Roger Dale Coad**

Copy Editor: **Cynthia L. McNew**

Audio: **Mark Garrow**

THE INDIANAPOLIS STAR
A Gannett Newspaper

President and Publisher: **Barbara A. Henry**

Editor and Vice President: **Terry Eberle**

Assistant Managing Editor/Sports: **Tim Wheatley**

Sports Editor: **Jim Lefko**

Assistant Managing Editor/Photography: **Charlie Nye**

Director of Photography: **Mike Fender**

Library Director: **Michael Jesse**

Assistant Library Director: **Cathy Knapp**

ISBN 1-58261-502-0

Table of Contents

Introduction

If the NASCAR popularity boom can be assigned a start date, it would be Nov. 15, 1992.

On that fall afternoon at Atlanta Motor Speedway, where the late Alan Kulwicki clinched the closest championship in Winston Cup history, one generation ended and another began.

As legendary Richard Petty made the last of his record 1,177 starts, 21-year-old Jeff Gordon made his first. Petty had made stock car racing a regional phenomenon for 40 years, but it was Gordon who in the next 10 years would take it national.

Buoyed by the expertise of crew chief Ray Evernham and the resources of team owner Rick Hendrick, Gordon earned his first Winston Cup championship in just his third full season. By 2002, when as a race car driver he was just entering his prime, he had three more championships and 58 wins, seventh on NASCAR's all-time list.

Growing up in Vallejo, Calif., Gordon aspired to race Indy cars, and his family moved to Pittsboro, Ind., to help him in that quest. But when he was ready to move up, he found the doors to Indy car racing closed. So he turned his attention southward and discovered opportunity in NASCAR.

In 1994, his dream to race at Indianapolis Motor Speedway was realized when NASCAR ran the first Brickyard 400. It became Gordon's second career win, and he has since won it twice more.

His rapid success, boyish good looks and Boy Scout reputation made him a polarizing force among fans and fellow competitors alike. But whether those fans came to root for or against him, they came—providing the impetus for NASCAR to take its show national with a number of new speedways in previously untapped markets from New England to Chicago to Texas to Las Vegas to Southern California. The sport's first network television deal arrived in 2001.

Although Gordon continues to elicit passionate response, positive and negative, from the grandstands, his acceptance among his rivals was sealed in 1995 by the man who stood to lose the most by Gordon's ascension, the late Dale Earnhardt.

Earnhardt dubbed the newcomer "Wonder Boy" and said that if he ever won a championship he would have to celebrate it drinking milk instead of champagne.

At the season-ending awards banquet in New York honoring Gordon's first title, he stood on the stage at the Waldorf-Astoria and raised a glass of milk in Earnhardt's direction. The seven-time Winston Cup champion stood and with a wide grin returned the salute.

Steve Ballard
The Indianapolis Star

Jeff Gordon
Career Highlights

1992

Gordon's first career Winston Cup start was on November 15 at Atlanta Motor Speedway. The race coincidentally was Richard Petty's final Winston Cup event.

1993

Jeff was Maxx Race Cards Rookie of the Year in the Winston Cup Series, becoming the first driver to win rookie honors in NASCAR's two top divisions (Busch Series, 1991). He won the 125-mile qualifying race at Daytona in February and was the first rookie in 30 years to accomplish that feat.

1994

Gordon won two Winston Cup Series races, including the inaugural Brickyard 400 at Indianapolis Motor Speedway and NASCAR's longest race, the Coca-Cola 600, at Charlotte Motor Speedway. He won more prize money ($1,607,010) than any NASCAR driver during the 31-race season and had seven top five and 14 top 10 finishes.

1995

Gordon became the youngest Winston Cup Series champion in NASCAR's modern era in only his third full season. He had seven victories, eight poles, 23 top 10 finishes, 2,610 laps led and $4,347,343 in overall winnings—the most ever by any NASCAR driver.

1996

Gordon finished with 10 victories, five poles, 2,313 laps led and had regular season earnings of $2,484,518 to lead in all those categories. He finished second in championship points, only 37 behind teammate Terry Labonte.

1997

Jeff won the 1997 NASCAR Winston Cup championship. He had 10 victories, one pole, 22 top five and 23 top 10 finishes. He became the youngest driver to win the Daytona 500 and the second driver to win the "Winston Million." Gordon broke regular season and overall earning records, becoming the only driver in NASCAR history to exceed $4 million in regular season winnings, and he passed the $6 million mark in overall earnings.

1998

Gordon won the 1998 NASCAR Winston Cup championship. He had 13 victories, seven poles, 26 top five and 28 top 10 finishes. He became the first driver to win the Brickyard 400 twice, and he won the "Winston No Bull Five" twice. He tied two modern-era records with 13 wins in one season and four wins in a row. Gordon won a record $6,175,867 in regular season earnings and over $9 million in overall earnings.

1999

Gordon became the youngest driver to win the Daytona 500 twice and finished the 1999 season with seven victories, becoming the first driver to win the most races for five straight years. He also won the most poles, with seven, and led the most laps, with 1,320. He finished the season sixth in points and had 18 top five and 21 top 10 finishes.

2000

Gordon became the youngest driver in Winston Cup history to achieve 50 career wins. He won three races in 2000, at Talladega, Richmond and Sears Point, where he set a record for six straight road course victories. He also tallied 11 top five and 21 top 10 finishes, along with three poles. He finished ninth in Winston Cup points.

2001

Gordon won the 2001 Winston Cup championship, becoming only the third driver to win four championships in a career. He led the Winston Cup Series in several statistical categories: wins (6), poles (6), top fives (18), top 10s (24), races led (25) and laps led (2,032). He became the first Winston Cup driver to eclipse $10 million in single season prize winnings. Gordon also won both The Winston and the Brickyard 400 for a third time.

2002

So far, Gordon has earned nearly $4 million in single season winnings. Even though the year didn't get off to his best start. After the Daytona 500 Jeff was ninth in the Winston Cup points race. By the fourth race in Atlanta he had fallen from the top 10. Of course that was only a temporary misstep. Jeff was back in the top five and was mounting a serious challenge for yet another championship.

Jeff Gordon celebrates an extra $1 million for winning the "No Bull Five" at the Brickyard 400 in 1998. Starting from third position, Gordon led 97 of 160 laps and led Mark Martin across the finish line as the race finished under yellow for the second time. Gordon became the first three-time winner in 2001. In six of the first nine Brickyard 400s, Gordon has won either the pole or the race.

Photo by Mike Fender

Jeff Gordon, 17, awaits the start of a sprint car race on July 29, 1989, in Winchester, Ind. Like many young men fresh out of high school, Gordon dreamed of hurtling around the Indianapolis Motor Speedway track at 200-plus miles per hour in the 500-Mile Race. Gordon was a resident of Pittsboro, Ind., and turned 18 on Aug. 4, 1989, several days after this picture was taken.

Photo by Jim Young

Relocation helps Gordon move full speed ahead

Zach Dunkin, Wednesday, June 21, 1989

Jeff Gordon dreams of racing in the 500-Mile Race someday, and his family moved halfway across the country to help him pursue that goal.

When Gordon was 15 and living in Vallejo, Calif., he needed a place to race sprint cars. A person has to be of legal driving age, 16, to drive sprint cars in California, but Gordon knew of some tracks in the Midwest without that restriction.

So he and his family—his mother and stepfather—left the San Francisco area, headed east, and landed in Pittsboro, Ind.

Now, it is common for American families to relocate because of a father's occupation, but for the career needs of a teenaged son?

"I guess they have a lot of faith in my future as a racer," said Gordon, who will compete in Thursday night's USAC midget race at Indianapolis Raceway Park. "We really work hard at it. I want to make it all the way to NASCAR or Indy car."

Gordon started racing at age five, when his stepfather, John Bickford, bought him a quarter-midget. Bickford had been around racing for a long time as a mechanic and now owns a company in California that makes parts for sprint cars and midgets.

Gordon won more than 300 races and two national championships in his quarter-midget before stepping into a sprint car at age 14.

"The quarter-midget thing was nothing serious at first," said Gordon, a graduate of Tri-West High School who won't turn 18 until Aug. 4. "It was something to play around with, but when we did well we started getting serious about it. One thing led to another."

Gordon got his USAC sprint car license last year and competed in a few USAC events before traveling to New Zealand over Christmas vacation with sprint car owner John Rae.

"It just started clicking. Getting over the scary feeling of the horsepower, how light the car was compared to the horsepower, and knowing the car was going to stick when I threw it into the corner. Once I got over that, there was nothing that was going to stop us."

—Jeff Gordon (at age 13)

Jeff Gordon, 17, of Pittsboro, Ind., and his stepfather, John Bickford, discuss how an accident knocked Jeff out of a race at Indianapolis Raceway Park.

Jeff Gordon, 17, of Pittsboro, Ind., leaves Indianapolis Raceway Park after a race with friends Angie Wilson (left) and Jonelle Riddle, both of Pittsboro.

Photo by Jim Young

He was quite successful there, winning about 80 percent of his races, according to Gordon. He also got his first taste as a full-scale midget racer.

Last month he took about five laps around the IRP oval in a friend's midget and decided to compete in the annual Night Before the 500 event there. He won the race.

"A lot of people were surprised, but I'm sure they weren't as surprised as I was," said Gordon, driving for Rollie Helmling. "After five years of racing in the sprint car, naturally, I feel more comfortable in it than the midget car, but I've got a lot of confidence in the car. I feel we can win some more races."

Thursday's race will be the second of the six-event USAC Jolly Rancher midget series at IRP and will be televised by ESPN.

The entry list includes veteran Rich Vogler, who finished eighth in last month's 500-Mile Race, USAC midget points leader Ross Gamester, 1987 USAC midget champion Kevin Olson and former 500 drivers Mel Kenyon and Stan Fox.

"He came out of the turn with the back end hanging out. I told the guy with me that I wanted to wait a minute and see him bust his tail. But I stood there for 20 laps, and he just kept on going. He was on the ragged edge all day." Gordon would go on to win the race that day. Rick Hendrick asked who the driver was. The response: "That Gordon kid." He then asked Jimmy Johnson, general manager of Hendrick Motorsports, to sign the driver to a contract: whatever it took. And the rest is history.

Jeff Gordon, 17, of Pittsboro, Ind., races in a sprint car race on July 29, 1989, in Winchester, Ind.

Photo by Jim Young

Pittsboro's Jeff Gordon making tracks

Staff Report, Friday, August 4, 1989

Like many 18-year-olds fresh out of high school, Jeff Gordon dreams of hurtling around the Indianapolis Motor Speedway track at 200-plus miles per hour in the 500-Mile Race.

Gordon, who turned 18 today, set a track record of 21.639 seconds (114.127 miles per hour) in the USAC midget event on the Hardee's Deluxe Racing Series schedule Thursday night at Indianapolis Raceway Park.

A resident of Pittsboro, Ind., Gordon knocked a thousandth of a second off the standard set on July 6 by Don Schilling.

The young driver, one of USAC's rising stars this season, took the early point lead in the sprint standings after his triumph in the May 20 series opener at Florence, Ky. He later added a victory in the Night Before the 500 at IRP.

Seeking an opportunity to race, Gordon moved to Indiana from Vallejo, Calif., when he was 15—too young to compete in California but not so at certain tracks in this state.

He began racing at age five when his stepfather, John Bickford, bought him a quarter-midget.

Gordon won more than 300 races and two national championships in his quarter-midget before moving up to sprint cars at age 14.

The graduate of Tri-West High School earned his USAC sprint car license last year.

His goal is to eventually move up to the Indy car class and compete at the Indianapolis Motor Speedway.

Considering the rapid climb he has made up the racing ladder, that day might be in the not-too-distant future.

"He came to my father's driving school. [After one] night, he called his mom, and said, 'Mom, I've made up my mind what I want to do with the rest of my life.' He wanted Winston Cup cars. As far as Indy racing goes, that was a kick in the pants for them. Because stars like him don't come along that often."

—Buddy Baker, NASCAR legend

Jeff Gordon (right) talks with team owner Bill Davis before the running of a Busch Grand National race at Indianapolis Raceway Park.

Photo by Greg Griffo

Gordon driving in a new fast lane

Curt Cavin, Sunday, December 9, 1990

Jeff Gordon knows where he's been in his short racing career and certainly knows where he's going.

He says, in a nutshell, that his eyes are wide open for his new venture. And that's no public relations talk.

The unassuming and likeable Gordon will sign a contract this week to become a full-time stock car driver. He'll race in NASCAR's Busch Grand National series, but believe him, it's hardly the minor leagues.

In the past four months, the 19-year-old Gordon has tested life in NASCAR's fast lane. He settled into Hugh Connerty's car three times this season and motored his way to the outside of Row 1 at Rockingham, N.C. Row 1, for heaven's sake.

The race was another matter. Quickly, the Boys of the South had the naïve Hoosier heading backward. Before long, Gordon was concrete-bound.

"A lack of experience on my part," Gordon said Friday.

That's the key for the reigning United States Auto Club midget champion. He has shown marvelous talent in driving Salem and Winchester, but Daytona and Dover are quite another matter. No open wheels mean no open space.

Jeff Gordon checks over his car before a Busch Grand National race at Indianapolis Raceway Park.

Photo by Greg Griffo

17

Jeff Gordon drives the Bill Davis Racing Ford into the pits after a crash in the running of a Busch Grand National race at Indianapolis Raceway Park.

Photo by Greg Griffo

"[Jeff] was trying to grow a mustache at the time, and when he opened his briefcase, he had a video game and a racing magazine in it," Ray Evernham said laughing. Few would have thought at the time that the two would later team up to become one of the most successful driver-crew chief combinations that the sport had ever seen.

"I really wasn't ready for it," he admitted. "You're out there with 30-40 cars, all nose to tail, side by side, rubbin' fenders. It's a totally different atmosphere. It isn't like being out there by yourself, believe me.

"We shocked a lot of people [with qualifying], but not ourselves. We had a good motor, though we didn't know about the car. But like I said, I can get a [stock car] to run pretty quick by myself. The racing part is something I've got to work on."

Gordon will have that chance with one of the better teams on the Grand National circuit. The Ford Thunderbird is co-owned by Connerty (of Jacksonville, Fla.) and Bill Davis (of Batesville, Ark.). The team's previous driver was Mark Martin.

The team will continue to have Carolina Ford Dealers' primary sponsorship while another investor could be on the way as early as next week. That financial mix should allow Gordon to compete for Rookie of the Year honors next season, which is the team's current goal.

If Tuesday is any indication, the 1991 collaboration could be interesting. During Goodyear radial tire testing at Rockingham, Gordon was reportedly quickest of the three drivers on hand.

"It's a great ride for me, a top 10 ride," Gordon said. "I never dreamed I'd have this kind of situation this early in my stock car career." Gordon says his team expects to compete in most of the Grand National events next season but not all. The rookie standings are based on a driver's best 15 appearances, which means running everywhere isn't necessary. Being selective will keep the team from being overwhelmed by its rookie relationship.

Gordon's resume is already rich in success despite his youth. Since breaking into USAC sprints in 1988, he's recorded five sprint and 11 midget feature victories. He won three consecutive events this season en route to the midget championship.

As the 1990 season came to a close, many wondered if Gordon would again drive a Midwest midget or sprinter. Some thought his ride today in the California Racing Association season sprint would be his finale with open wheels.

Apparently, it won't. His '90 rides will be available on an as-needed basis, so when NASCAR takes a break, Gordon won't.

"I still want to drive midgets and sprints when I can," he said. "I still have a lot to learn."

Jeff Gordon (right) talks with his team owner Bill Davis before the running of a Busch Grand National race at Indianapolis Raceway Park. The car is owned by Davis, of Batesville, Ark. (shown with Gordon), and Hugh Connerty of Jacksonville, Fla., and the team's previous driver was Mark Martin.

Photo by Greg Griffo

Jeff Gordon at his first Winston Cup race at Atlanta in November 1992.

Gordon groomed for success

Staff Report, Friday, February 19, 1993

Among the maddening crowd surrounding NASCAR's newest hero last Sunday were the only two people who know how far, and fast, Jeff Gordon has traveled in his 21 years.

And, as Gordon readily volunteers, the two folks who made his racing career a reality instead of a dream.

"Can anybody have a better life than me?" gushed Gordon after starting third, leading and finishing fifth in last Sunday's Daytona 500. "I'm so thankful to everyone who's helped me get here, but nobody more than my mom and dad.

"They made it all possible."

What Carol and John Bickford did for their son goes way beyond a father playing catch with his son in the backyard or a mother encouraging her little girl's first bicycle solo without training wheels.

The Bickfords gave Gordon a parent's normal nurturing and a loving environment, but they also provided a rare opportunity for a teenager to start a profession while most kids are still trying to find summer jobs.

Jeff Gordon, 21, NASCAR driver, photographed April 30, 1993.

Photo by Greg Griffo

"So much of my life is spent just focused on driving race cars, driving race cars; win, win, win; lose-win, lose-win, [but] it's not always about that. There's a lot more to life than that and I'm fortunate that I get to give back at times."

—Jeff Gordon

They put Jeff on the right track, literally and figuratively, and he's rewarded them with instant success, miles of maturity and an inner pride that can't be defined.

"Right after the race, it was tough to get near Jeff, but I managed to give him a hug and ask, 'Did you pinch yourself yet? This really isn't a dream,'" said John Bickford, who married Carol when Jeff was three years old.

"I mean, we knew he was good, but I don't think anybody was ready for this."

Maybe not ready for such sudden success amongst stock car racing's elite, but certainly prepared.

From his early days (five years old) in quarter-midgets, to go-karts and then the decision to try sprint cars at 13, Jeff never drove anything he wasn't ready for.

"Before Jeff began racing quarter-midgets, I found an old field full of weeds, dug it up and made a track," said Bickford, whose business and home were then located in Vallejo, Calif. "He slid around for hours getting used to that car and he probably had 50,000 laps.

"We also got Carol a quarter-midget, and she'd run against him, practicing starts, snookering him in the corners and teaching him how to react. She was a driving force, for sure."

There weren't enough quarter-midget races for Jeff's age group, so the Bickfords built a go-kart. Jeff was then able to run both classes on the same day, scrambling back and forth and winning 60 consecutive kart shows.

By the time Jeff was 13, he was looking for a new challenge because he'd mastered quarter-midgets and go-karts.

"I'd heard about this 14-year-old named Sport Allen who was running sprinters in Florida," said Bickford. "We checked it out and found out it was true, so I asked Jeff if he wanted to try it and he was all fired up."

Considering the lethal nature of sprinters, putting a 13-year-old son into one sounds like an advanced case of child abuse. That was the reaction John got upon arriving at Lee Osborne's race shop in Jamestown, Ind., in 1985.

"I told Lee I was interested in a sprinter, and he said, 'Aren't you kinda old to be starting a sprint car career?'" recalled Bickford, who was 38 at the time. "I replied it wasn't for me but for Jeff.

Jeff Gordon sits in his DuPont Chevy after crashing out of his first Winston Cup race at Atlanta in November 1992.

Photo by Greg Griffo

"Lee looked at Jeff and said something like, 'Get outta here. I'm not gonna build a sprinter for a child.' But we were finally able to talk him into it, and all he had to do was build a special seat."

So the kid who looked even younger than 13 1/2 began running sprinters, with his dad turning the wrenches and his mom staying in California running the business. From '85 through '88 he ran over 400 races at dirt tracks all over the Midwest, running against guys like Ricky Hood, Danny Smith and the Kinsers.

"He really matured quickly running against those guys," said Bickford, who moved the family to Pittsboro in July 1986.

A full-time ride in the World of Outlaws in 1989 began with a victory on the pavement at Sandusky, Ohio, but ended with Jeff being released and told he wasn't quite fast enough to keep up with his equipment.

"That was a turning point in Jeff's career," continued Bickford. "He was devastated because someone had told him he wasn't good enough. But I told him the only person he had to please was Jeff Gordon.

"Plus, he didn't get stuck in that old rut like so many USAC guys have."

Gordon began focusing on asphalt. He drove a Super Vee at IRP, went to Buck Baker's school for stockers and hopped into a USAC midget, where he promptly debuted with a victory in the Night Before the 500 event at IRP.

He captured the USAC midget title in 1990 but got everyone's attention down south by qualifying on the outside of the front row in his NASCAR Busch Grand National debut at Rockingham, N.C.

From there it was on to a full-time Busch ride in '91 and '92 before Rick Hendrick signed him on the dotted line last May for what promises to be an awesome run in Winston Cup.

"I miss Jeff a lot and so does his mother, but we're so proud of him," said Bickford, who plans to make about half the NASCAR races. "Watching him go from quarter-midgets to leading the Daytona 500... There's no way I can describe that."

How about good grooming?

Pittsboro, Indiana's Jeff Gordon made his homecoming a memorable one. He waves to fans at the Indianapolis Motor Speedway as he comes to the first Brickyard 400, to be held on August 6, 1994.

Photo by Kerry Keating

Hoosier-groomed Jeff Gordon has taken NASCAR by storm, sending him to the Brickyard . . .

On a FAST TRACK

Dick Mittman, Saturday, July 30, 1994

It was the Wednesday before the Talladega 500 stock car race, and young NASCAR driving sensation Jeff Gordon had to be in Tupelo, Miss., for a special occasion.

A commercial flight from Charlotte, N.C., would get him home late that night—but not in time to make the party for the third birthday of crew chief Ray Evernham's son, Ray Jr., who was suffering from leukemia.

So Gordon chartered a plane at his own expense to fly him to Tupelo and back.

"Jeff's very close with him [Ray Jr.]," said the senior Evernham. "This is not a business deal. It's friendship."

This is another behind-the-scenes story about the Hoosier-groomed driver who has taken NASCAR racing by storm. In just two years he has become a favorite in a sport where drivers with open-wheel backgrounds seldom excel.

On his 23rd birthday Thursday, the Tri-West High School graduate will be at the Indianapolis Motor Speedway attempting to qualify for the Brickyard 400, the most widely anticipated new automobile race since the Marmon Wasp stung 39 other competitors in the first Indianapolis 500-Mile Race in 1911.

Along with stars like Dale Earnhardt, Ernie Irvan and Rusty Wallace, Gordon will be among top choices to take the checkered flag and have his name forever remembered, like Ray Harroun's, as a first-time winner of a storied event at the historic track.

"He's certainly made a big impact on the sport," said Ned Jarrett, a Hall of Fame driver and now a racing commentator.

"It was obvious when he was in Grand National racing that he had a tremendous amount of talent. He has the right attitude, good looks, is articulate. Those attributes will carry him along."

Question: What's the key to winning at Talladega?

Jeff: "A lot of luck. You're lucky just to get out of there in one piece, so it obviously takes a lot of luck to win. I don't know what it's going to be like this time. The rules are a little bit different than they were when we were there last time, so we're just going to have to wait and see how you've got to race and how you've got to race with those rules."

"Talladega and Daytona are almost as different as Bristol and Charlotte. It's hard to imagine because there's only almost two-tenths of a mile difference between the two. Handling at Daytona is very important, and at Talladega it means absolutely nothing. I think that's why it's a little bit tougher for us at Talladega, because at Daytona, handling is a component that we can utilize. We have typically handled real good at Daytona like we did this year."

—Jeff Gordon

On Friday at Talladega, Ala., Superspeedway, his crew swarmed over his brightly painted Chevrolet Lumina to prepare it for practice and qualifying for Sunday's 500-mile race, the last one before the Brickyard.

Joining Evernham were Patrick Donahue, Brian Whitesell, Ed Guzzo, Shawn Parker and Dave Tatman.

As Evernham awaited Gordon's arrival, he discussed the driver he first teamed with in the Grand National series, a training ground for those planning to race in Winston Cup. Gordon moved to NASCAR after winning the USAC midget title and then added the Silver Crown dirt car crown while winning the Grand National Rookie of the Year award.

"We did a deal in October 1990," Evernham said. "The first time I saw him he was 17 and looked 13. I said, 'My, God, what did I get myself into?'

"But after his first few laps [at Charlotte] I knew I had a real talent. He got sideways at 170 and straightened it up without a bobble and brought it in. Right then I knew I had a race driver."

A couple of stalls down, Irvan talked about the bright newcomer.

"Jeff's going to be consistent," Irvan said. "His only downfall is he didn't grow up building race cars. You look at the guys who win most of the races and they all grew up working on them."

It was time to start practice. Gordon pulled on his multicolored helmet and soon had his car winging around the high-banked oval.

Gordon returned the car a second time to the cover of the open garage—to permit the engine to cool because of the intense Alabama heat. Engine man David Tatman lifted the hood and peered into the motor compartment.

"He's a heck of a nice guy and he's going to be a future champion," said Tatman. "He is a lot of fun. We laugh and joke around. But he's smart, real smart. He's got a good head on his shoulders."

Jeff Gordon, in the DuPont car, swapped the lead with Ernie Irvan four times before capturing the victory in the inaugural Brickyard 400 at the Indianapolis Motor Speedway.

Indianapolis News Photo

Less than two months ago, the day of the Indianapolis 500, Gordon won the Coca-Cola 600 at Charlotte. He had stunned the racing world by winning a 125-mile qualifying race at Daytona International Speedway in his 1993 NASCAR debut, but this was his first feature victory. It came in his 42nd NASCAR race.

Bearded Bill Brodrick of Unocal 76 was there to put the winner's hat on him, just as he had for hundreds of other NASCAR race champions.

Ray Evernham and Jeff Gordon

Photo by Paul Sancya

"I think so far his biggest asset is that he has kept his head screwed on straight," Brodrick said.

When Talladega practice was over, Gordon stood in front of his transporter and patiently endured seven media interviews.

Finally, Gordon slipped to the sanctuary of the room in the front of the transporter.

In late afternoon his car was in qualifying line, the No. 43 Pontiac that Richard Petty once drove so splendidly in front of him and Dale Earnhardt's No. 3 Chevy behind.

"I really don't see him being another anybody," Evernham said. "He's the first Jeff Gordon, a trendsetter."

At 4 p.m. Gordon climbed easily through the driver's window and began tightening his straps. Earnhardt leaned in and talked for a minute—"we were discussing his new motor home," Earnhardt said with a laugh—and then Gordon fired the engine and moved away.

Linda Sims of Alabasta, Ala., a member of the track medical staff, cheered.

"He's not afraid to take chances," she said of Gordon, her favorite driver. "He reminds me of Davey Allison. Like in the race in May, he started 40th and he's soon up in the top 10."

Gordon turned his first lap at 190.370 mph, then hiked it to 190.806. It was good for only 15th place. He made some nice comments over the public address system and left the track.

Saturday dawned hot and muggy. Gordon practiced and then spotted for Ricky Craven, a DuPont driver, in the Grand National race. Gordon stayed in his new motor home with fiancee Brooke Sealey, playing video games and eating a lunch she prepared. They will be married Nov. 25 in Charlotte.

In the transporter, Gordon's parents, John and Carol Bickford, talked about his success. John took Carol to a race on their first date when Jeff was one. He had Jeff racing go-karts at age five. When Jeff was 13 the family moved from California to Indiana so he would have a better opportunity to drive midgets and sprinters in USAC.

John called himself a delegator of duties. He drives the motor home, works with the fan club and does whatever else is needed. Russ and Maureen Harris of Williams, Ariz., organized the fan club in 1992 with 27 members. The total is up to 5,000 now.

"What people have to consider is that this is not something that just came on," Bickford said. "Jeff started racing 18 seasons ago. That's a little different than someone who starts at 20 at Bloomington Speedway. Fans are looking for someone new."

Evernham sees Gordon as a trendsetter. "He's the first Jeff Gordon... I really don't see him being another anybody," Evernham said.

Photo by Steven Noreyko

Jeff Gordon poses by his car. He went on to win the first NASCAR race at the Indianapolis Motor Speedway.

Photo by Scott Sady

Bickford admitted he's a little overwhelmed when he thinks about it.

And Jeff's mother says, "I can't say this is the life we dreamed of. When he was racing quarter-midgets, we didn't think about Winston Cup racing. When we moved to Indiana others were thinking about Indy.

"It took a couple of years of racing in sprint cars before we thought about how far he could go. It was the late 1980s that his life started to change drastically."

John called Gordon's "college" the racetracks at places like Winchester and DuQuoin. He said Jeff began to specialize like a doctor might when he joined the Grand National series.

"Now he's in graduate school," he said. "A lot of dreamers confuse dollars with effort."

The sun beat fiercely down on race morning. In the Jeff Gordon souvenir trailer, Bill Henry of Concord, N.C., perspired as he sold T-shirts and other items but wished he was on the outside of the track, where customer traffic is even heavier.

"They do good, real good," he commented about sales to fans.

Back at the front of the transporter, John Bickford talked about the marketing popularity of his stepson. He said it is No. 2 in the industry.

"We have three trailers with five people working in each of them. The most popular shirt is the one for his first win. Second is the 'Ready to Rumble' shirt with bricks on the back."

As the cars are pushed out to the starting grid, pace car driver Elmo Langley, a NASCAR driver for many years, said he likes the way Gordon handles himself.

"He's probably as talented a young driver as has come along in a long while," he remarked.

Added Les Richter, NASCAR vice president: "I hope he keeps his head right through all this. So far he seems to think before he makes any remarks."

Moon-walking astronaut Buzz Aldrin told the drivers to "energize their landcraft" and the race was under way. Gordon quickly moved through the pack to join the front runners. He stayed there until his engine blew at the start of the 150th lap.

"Things had been going great all weekend, but it just didn't last long enough," Gordon said.

On Monday Jeff and Brooke were back at his townhouse on Lake Norman near Charlotte. It was time to get away from the tension building for the Brickyard.

Tuesday was another day for relaxation, but when his public relations man, Ron Miller, told him a writer wanted an interview, he said he would call as soon as he finished lunch.

"[Those people] have no idea about Jeff sleeping in the back of his truck because he couldn't drive the diesel down the freeway, about making belly pans and selling them at the racetrack because we were holding on to every dime."
—John Bickford, Jeff's stepfather, on Jeff's early racing days and critics

In 1994 autographs were a priority for these Tower Terrace fans at the practice for the first Brickyard 400.

Photo by Rich Miller

True to his word, the call came right on time.

Gordon said he never expected to get as far as he has. He said he takes things one race at a time and that when he went the NASCAR route he felt running at the speedway would never again be on his agenda.

"Now nothing seems to amaze me," he said.

He has not allowed, as many competitors have noted, his skyrocketing rise to fame to

change his helmet size.

"I think there is a big difference between being confident and being cocky," he explained. "I feel very confident in my ability and in my team.

"My concentration is not on making a lot of money and getting bigger headlines. I don't live a glamorous life though I'm in a glamorous business."

He admits he has the money to buy first-class things, but he doesn't flaunt it.

Gordon drives a vehicle provided every three months by Chevrolet. He has use of a Mark III van for a year. Lee Osborn of Jamestown, his car builder when he was driving in USAC, is building street rods for him and his father. His personal car is a Lexus that is two years old and barely has 8,000 miles on the odometer.

Because of his racing commitments, Gordon says he didn't make many close friends in high school. But two of those friends are brothers Brad and Brian Hawkins. Brad will be in his wedding.

"My closest friend is Brooke," Gordon said.

Next week Gordon will be back in the whirlwind with appearances early in the week. Then come the three most exciting days of his young life, the practice, qualifying and running of the Brickyard 400.

"It's going to be more hectic than any race that we've been to," he said. "I'm going to enjoy it very much."

36

All 43 drivers line up for introductions at the Indianapolis Motor Speedway for the inaugural Brickyard 400.

Photo by Kristin Enzor

Months of exercise in the weight room have made Jeff Gordon a more formidable opponent.

Photo by Kerry Keating

Gordon is big-time but not big-headed

Curt Cavin, Thursday August 4, 1994

Former Hoosier sprinter is busier but otherwise unchanged by success.

The first change is the upper lip. Last year he wielded a razor beneath his nose and sliced off that wiry black mustache that had aged his appearance by at least three years.

Then came the extra strength added to his ever-tiny frame (5'7", 140 pounds). Months of exercise in the weight room have made him stronger. He's more seasoned and more, dare we say, warrior-like.

There have been other changes to Jeff Gordon, who left Indiana as a two-time U.S. Auto Club champion in 1991 for a shot at stock car racing. No longer is he fighting for his piece of the small-time pie. Last year's national fan voting (through McDonald's) placed him with Dale Earnhardt and Rusty Wallace as the most popular drivers on the nation's most popular auto racing circuit. Gordon, who celebrates his 23rd birthday today, is more rich and famous than he could ever have imagined.

Strangely, it does not show when he looks in the mirror. For all of the breaks and good advice he has received in the sport, he was taught an exhaustive lesson in reality at home.

His mother and stepfather, Carol and John Bickford, have walked virtually every step of his career with a shepherd's cane. They have insisted he be generous with the media and the fans. They have groomed his public speaking, helping him become one of the most easygoing and enlightening interviews simply by being himself.

Through all the hype of being NASCAR's latest star, Gordon has remained level-headed and roots-respecting. Ask him a question and wait for a cooperative answer.

The only difference between the Gordon of pre-stardom and the Gordon of today is that now he has less time. Every minute of business is spent catering to the expectations of the masses.

"I really admire him. I think he's without a doubt the greatest driver that's come along in several years, and it just amazes me sometimes to see some of the things he can do."
—Terry Labonte on teammate Jeff Gordon

Fans check out Jeff Gordon as he exits the garage area. Jeff is constantly pursued for pictures or autographs by his fans.   Photo by Paul Sancya

"It's got to be one of the biggest, most successful rises in racing history," said Ron Miller, who co-ordinates Gordon's schedule with lead sponsor DuPont. Miller has been involved with NASCAR since starting as a newspaper reporter in 1964, seven years before Gordon was born in Vallejo, Calif.

"Jeff's a great person and his head is on straight," Miller said. "Put any other 22-year-old sitting where he's sitting and see what happens. Hell, put me in that situation and see what happens."

When Gordon makes a mistake on the racetrack, he admits it—usually promptly. When he reaches victory lane, as he did at Charlotte last month, he follows his emotions. The

Coca-Cola 600 was his first Winston Cup victory in 42 starts. When he got to the awards stand, he wept. And wept.

"It was pretty unexpected," he said of the triumph and tears. "My emotions took over and the world saw it."

So did boyhood friend Stevie Reeves, who has raced against Gordon too many times to count, beginning in quarter-midgets. A few weeks ago Gordon was testing at Indianapolis Motor Speedway. The former area residents had lunch and erased the miles that had separated them during three race-filled years with one very ordinary pal session.

"To me, there's no change in Jeff whatsoever," said Reeves, a rookie in NASCAR's Busch Grand National series. "[The lack of time] is the business, not Jeff. Being around him some down here [on the southern circuit], I can't imagine what he has to go through every night, going to dinner and constantly being hounded for his autograph while he's trying to eat.

"He doesn't act like he should or could, you know what I mean? He doesn't take all of this [success and attention] for granted because he's earned it. It's hard for people to see that. They think he's changed, but really they've changed in the way they look at him."

These days, many people get looks at Gordon, a sponsor's dream on and off the track. He and his family thought the off-track time might slow down with only 31 Winston Cup races, compared with the 95 races he ran yearly in open-wheel cars. Not so. It seems every day starts at 6 a.m. with a map-out session, a plane trip somewhere, lunch on the run, autographs, speaking engagements and few shut-eye moments. Breaks are what he takes out of necessity.

"All those laps in sprint and midgets cars helped make Jeff what he is today. You learn something about your competitors with every lap, anticipating what they do. Everyone's amazed when he avoids a crash, but that's not an accident. He's never broken a bone that I know of, never spent a night in a hospital. When he was 10 at Hills Ferry Speedway in California, someone ran over him with a go-kart and I took a piece of the fence off and used it as a splint for his shoulder. He was sore, but he wanted to race."
—John Bickford, Jeff's stepfather

NASCAR driver Jeff Gordon signs autographs at the 31 South Shopping Center in Indianapolis as his fiancee, Brooke, watches. The line for autographs went out the store and around the building.

Photo by Paul Sancya

"Nothing in life is free," said John Bickford, "and if you've got a $2 million sponsor, they expect something in return. It's not just TV time."

"There are no weeks off," said Carol Bickford, who handles most of her son's business with her husband. "Jeff works every single day and he spends very few days at home [in Huntersville, N.C.]."

Besides the change in work there has been a change in lifestyle. The day he won the prestigious Busch Clash as part of the 1993 Daytona 500, he was introduced to series trophy girl Brooke Sealey. Several Winston Cup veterans had tried to get the two introduced for weeks, but an opportunity had not been available.

In victory lane, the spark ignited. They went to dinner and got to know one another. Before long they were an item. Feb. 16, a year to the day after they met, Gordon proposed marriage. The outgoing Miss Winston accepted.

They will be wed Nov. 26 in Charlotte, her hometown.

Gordon and Sealey are virtually inseparable during the relaxing moments, playing video games religiously in the motor home at the track. They enjoy movies, dinner, riding bicycles, traveling.

Meanwhile, business rolls on. Miller has been so inundated with telephone calls requesting Gordon appearances that 1994 is booked.

"I'm still the same person but a whole lot busier and, obviously, the money's different," Gordon said.

Hoosier Jeff Gordon celebrates on top of his race car after winning the first NASCAR Brickyard 400 at the Indianapolis Motor Speedway on Saturday, Aug. 6, 1994. The 23-year-old driver lived in Pittsboro, Ind., from 1984 to 1991.

The kid shows 'em how

Dick Mittman, Monday, August 8, 1994

Youngest driver on NASCAR circuit shows the veterans how it is done.

Superstars—a Nolan Ryan, a Magic Johnson, a Joe Montana—come along only once every so often in sports. They have tremendous talent, an incredible desire to win and an amazing ability to perform at their peak in the biggest events.

Finally, they have special personal appeal out of uniform that draws fans by the droves. Dave Letterman wants them. So does *Good Morning, America*. Disney World beckons.

Saturday afternoon at the Indianapolis Motor Speedway in the inaugural Brickyard 400 NASCAR race, more than 250,000 fans and millions more on television witnessed the birth of sport's newest young superstar.

Jeff Gordon, a hometown boy just two days beyond his 23rd birthday, ran all of stock car's greats into the bricks—well, asphalt—and took the checkered flag for a history-making victory.

Then he climbed out of his brightly colored Chevrolet Lumina and eventually on top of it and boyishly celebrated like he was the winning pitcher in the Little League World Series.

He also said all the right things, posed for all the victory hat photographs, hugged his mother, kissed his fiancee and thanked his crew.

"He *is* a superstar," said Jim Perkins, who heads up Chevrolet's division of General Motors.

"Did you see how he ran down Ernie Irvan? That kid is relentless."

Ray Evernham, Gordon's crew chief and friend, saw him in a slightly different light.

"I don't think he wants to be a superstar, just a kid who wants to drive race cars good," Evernham said. "He's the best driver I've ever seen."

> "I don't feel I'm a step above anyone on this team. I'm just another link in the chain."
>
> —Jeff Gordon

Forty-three drivers thunder away on the first lap of the first Brickyard 400. The excitement of the start was matched by the finish, when Jeff Gordon fended off challengers to win by .53 seconds.

Photo by Tim Halcomb

Car owner Rick Hendrick, who is the Roger Penske of NASCAR, signed Gordon over two years ago after seeing him drive for the first time in a Grand National race. He thought the youngster was going to crash and watched in awe as Gordon drove lap after lap with smoking tires, but without a bobble.

"Jeff's got as much raw talent as any driver as I've ever seen," he exclaimed.

Stepfather John Bickford, part of the mob scene on the victory lift, doesn't look on Gordon's mercurial rise (the Brickyard follows his initial victory in the Coca-Cola 600 at Charlotte on May 29) as putting him in the superstar category.

"I just look on him as my kid," he said.

"Every guy who races is a superstar in someone's eyes. Racing at the speedway is the greatest honor you can bestow and his victory represents America."

Mother Carol, unconcerned about her son being elevated to special status, admitted she cried as he crossed the finish line.

"Happy tears; they're the best kind," she said.

Gordon, who learned his trade driving sprints and midgets while living in nearby Pittsboro, led 93 of the 160 laps.

The crowd was standing through the last 20 laps as Irvan, who overcame the nickname "Swervin' Irvan" to win the Daytona 500 and lead in the current NASCAR standings, and Gordon dueled mile after mile in front of the pack.

At one point, they drove nearly side by side through six turns. Irvan finally took the lead with 25 miles to go, but Gordon clung tenaciously to his rear bumper.

Then on lap 155 Irvan slowed in turn two and headed for the pits with a cut right front tire.

Gordon's car was loose and Brett Bodine was leading a fast-closing pack of four that included the indomitable Dale Earnhardt. The pressure was tremendous, but the budding superstar never faltered and whipped under the checkered flag 53 hundredths of a second in front of Bodine. He averaged 131.932 miles per hour.

Later in the press interview room he said he felt like a kid in a candy store. His emotions, he said, were far past any words he could bring forth.

"This is the Indianapolis 500 of stock cars," he said. "This one was built up so much. Everyone wanted to win this race. There wasn't anyone who wanted to win it more than us."

He said the advantage he had at the speedway was that it put everyone on equal ground because no one had raced a stock car there before. At the other tracks he had to contend with the experience of the veterans.

His closest calls involved Geoff Bodine, a tough challenger early in the race.

First they banged together as Gordon prepared to enter the pits, bending his left front fender. Later, Brett Bodine spun out his brother exiting turn four. Gordon dived low and got through before Geoff Bodine's car whipped back across the track and knocked out the less fortunate Dale Jarrett.

"The last 10 laps Ernie and I had a heck of a race," Gordon said.

"I wouldn't have wanted to fight Earnhardt either. I'm sorry he hit the wall [turn four on the first lap] . . . darn."

Gordon said he let Irvan lead because being in front was hard on the tires. He added that he charged as hard as he could with five laps to go to disturb the air around Irvan.

"If it had come to the last lap, we'd have been side by side. Our cars were that close."

In victory and before he knew he would pick up a check for a stock car record $613,000, Gordon talked modestly about how luck helped him in the race and in his career.

"There are a million kids out there with the same talent, but don't get that break," he said. "Rick Hendrick gave me a break."

But, as John Bickford noted, Gordon worked extremely hard for 18 years to receive that opportunity.

Superstars may appear to be instant successes, but it takes years of preparation to reach that point. Ask Larry Bird.

The Rainbow Warriors celebrate Jeff Gordon's win of the inaugural Brickyard 400.

Photo by Kristin Enzor

The Rainbow Warrior crew pushes the No. 24 DuPont Chevrolet driven by Jeff Gordon through the garage area at the Indianapolis Motor Speedway at the NASCAR Brickyard 400.

Photo by Paul Sancya

Gordon doesn't press for answers

Full news conference comments from the Brickyard 400's first winner, Jeff Gordon.

Q It's been an exciting hour for Jeff since this race is over, but Jeff, if you would, give us some general reaction to your victory today.

A Man, without tears coming up, hey, this is the greatest thing in the world. I know Ray (Evernham, team manager) is awfully happy. This whole team just has really done an excellent job to prepare for this. Far past our expectations, I know that. I never thought that would ever happen. It's a moment I've been waiting for for a long time, just to be a part of it. And to even think about being a winner of this event is far past anything we ever thought of.

I'll tell you, this is a great day. I hope that I'm here at the Indianapolis Speedway all day long. I'm in a candy store, I've got a big smile on my face. It's just great. I don't know what to say. It's just far past any words that can describe the way I feel. You know, to me this is the Indianapolis 500 of stock car racing today. I mean, this is the biggest event to date. And everybody's going to remember this. I'm just happy to be a part of it and definitely happy to be the winner. That's for sure.

Q Jeff, you know the history and heritage of this place after growing up so close to here, but you know the one indelible mark you left on it is you and Ray Harroun are always going to be mentioned as first-time winners of this place and that car's going to end up over in the museum. Talk about that a little bit.

A Well, as bad as my memory is, I still remember Ray Harroun's name so I guess that's a pretty good thing. Well, from my perspective, I don't know what it was like back in 1911. I think that's when he won that. I don't know if everybody participated in the race like they did this one, but this one was built up so much and so highly anticipated. And I think everybody wanted to win this race. You saw how many cars came to qualify, how close it was just to make the race. That just shows the determination of the guys that wanted to win this race. There wasn't anybody that wanted to win any worse than us obviously today, because we just had our act together. I'm just so glad we were on equal grounds. I think this was the first time in my NASCAR career that I was on equal grounds. And I think by saying that, I mean a racetrack that has no history of

1999—Jeff Gordon comments on all the anti-Gordon fan displays: "When you pull into victory lane," Gordon says confidently with a hint of irreverence in his voice, "it makes you feel good that you just ruined their day."

NASCAR races. It's so tough to go each and every weekend to some of these tracks that these guys have been racing on for so many years and try to hit that combination they have taken so many years to find. And Ray is one of the greatest at doing it when we were given that opportunity, you know, on equal grounds, he's the best, and we work well together and we just make a heck of a team. This is the first opportunity to do that and I think that's why we were fast today.

Q Help me remember this, three things: When you came into the pits and rubbed with Geoff Bodine, how close was that to going into the wall? Two, your view when Brett and Geoff (Bodine) got together? And three, take us through those last 10 laps.

A OK, let's see. The first one, I was out and just getting ready to come in and Geoff Bodine was coming out, and I passed him on the back straightaway. And as soon as I passed him, I knew he was going to be faster than me, he had new tires and all, I waved my hand in the short stretch. He thought, I actually don't know what he thought I was waving at, but I was waving to come in the pits. And I tried to get as low on the race track as I could and I think he might have thought I was blocking him, because he sure was blocking me when he was leading. So I thought I gave him enough room on the outside, but he tried to go to the inside and I didn't know he was coming. I think he just didn't know I was coming in the pits. It was very close. We actually rubbed and it bent our left front fender up. I don't know how

Jeff Gordon drives past a long line of crew members from other teams after winning the 1994 Brickyard 400 at the Indianapolis Motor Speedway.

Photo by Mike Fender

Jeff Gordon shakes hands with Indiana governor Evan Bayh as Indianapolis mayor Steve Goldsmith (center) looks on.

Photo by Rich Miller

much it hurt the car, but it did affect it a little bit, a little bit on the left front fender.

Let's see, number two, I didn't see what happened with Brett and Geoff at all. As a matter of fact, I asked Ray on the radio if somebody touched him, because it looked like it just took the air off him. So I don't know what happened there. All I know is he spun and I was trying to keep from hitting him. I didn't know if he was going to hit the wall, come down in front of me. You know, that's when you know it's your day when breaks like that happen and luck's on your side, the guy upstairs is on your side, just missing wrecks and things like that.

As far as the last 10 laps, Ernie and I, man, we had one heck of a race going. The last guy I wanted to race was Ernie at the end. He's so confident. But I guess I probably wouldn't want to be racing (Dale) Earnhardt either. I hated to see him hit the wall there on the first lap (laughter), because he would have put up a heck of a fight, I'm sure.

But Ernie was tough. When I was leading, he could get right up on me and loosen me up and I'd have to let him go right on by. The thing was, I could do the same thing to him. I could get right up on him and loosen him up. So we were just counting down at the laps, because it wasn't doing me any good to be in front of him because I was just wearing my tires out. I thought maybe I could help wear his tires out a little bit and wait there towards the end and get a run on him and make him work to pass me. That's, you know, what I did.

With four laps to go—I think it was four, five or four, five maybe—I drove as hard as I could in on him to try to get him loose going into the corner. Not to spin him or anything, just so he'd move up the track. Then he started moving up the track and I wasn't prepared for it. And then I saw him fall back and I said he had a right front go down. But I never touched him or anything. I was trying to get as much air off him as possible so I could get a run on him and pass him, but we had a heck of a race going. And I guarantee you it would have came down all the way to that last lap. We would have come across the line side by side. I don't know who would have won, because we had very equal cars at the end.

Q Jeff, four or five years ago you were running Saturday nights not too far from here. I was wondering if you ever thought you'd be where you are right now?

A Absolutely not. I don't even think I need to answer that one. There's no way I thought I was here, going to be here. I never thought I'd get to Winston Cup racing, first of all. There are so many steps along the way that had to be taken. Meeting Ray Evernham was one of the greatest moments that I didn't know about. He was involved in that first Busch Grand National car. It's so funny the way luck is on your side or the breaks that you get. There's a million kids out there the same age as me that have a lot of talent who just don't get the breaks. They're out there somewhere and I hope the car owners and sponsors continue to look for those guys, 'cause they're out there. They gave me a

Jeff Gordon takes off during practice for the 1994 Brickyard 400 at the Indianapolis Motor Speedway.

Photo by Mike Fender

55

Jeff Gordon drives past the yard of bricks and takes the checkered flag as the winner of the Brickyard 400 at the Indianapolis Motor Speedway.

Photo by Damon Winter

break, gave me an opportunity and I've been able to do something with it. Me and Ray were one of those things and we just stayed together, and we make a good team, we communicate and we're best friends. So that makes a big difference, but I never thought I would be racing for Rick Hendrick.

Kenny Schrader would come to race with me in an open-wheel car and he was like close to God. He wasn't God. Rick's God. It was like, man, here's Kenny Schrader. He's got a big sponsor from Winston Cup driving for Rick Hendrick. Rick Hendrick, like, he was the guy. Him and Roger Penske, they're the guys. So for that opportunity to come for me to drive for Rick, you know, and to have Ray on board to put people together and then DuPont came on board, I mean, it was a great moment in my life. And that was before they ever announced Indianapolis was going to happen, so I thought I had pretty much blown my chances of going Indy or my chances in the Indianapolis 500 are over with. And until Bill France and Tony George started talking, man, all I heard was rumors to begin with and I was trying to push them all the way. I was going, boy, I hope it happens, boy, I hope it happens. Every time I saw Tony I'd say, boy, I hope it happens; see Bill, boy, I hope it happens. It happened. And here we are.

Q We know you were pretty busy those last couple of laps. Do you have any idea how much the crowd was rooting for you? Number two, now that you're 23, do you no longer cry like at Charlotte?

A That's why I took an extra lap. Got all the tears wiped off my face. You know, I can't control my emotions. I still, when I really think about it, get caught up in it. You know, I don't want to be a cry baby all the time.

Charlotte was a great thrill. I wouldn't want any place but Charlotte to be my first win. And I wouldn't want any place to be my second win other than this one. I think winning that race prepared me for this one. I don't think a guy who has never won a race before is going to be able to come in here and do what we did. A lot of that was gaining that experience of one win at Charlotte. But I was actually emotional. If anybody had a scanner on they heard me screaming and yelling and all these guys. And I'm probably glad I couldn't hear the fans, because that would have made me choke up even more. I was just thrilled to death and I told myself, I'm not going to get emotional like I did, because I hyperventilated and needed oxygen last time. I didn't want that to happen.

Q A couple of things. First of all, you said that it really didn't do you any good to be out in front because Ernie was getting loose when you were behind, so why with five laps to go did you go to the front instead of waiting a little bit? The second thing is, you seemed to be able to deal with everybody else on the track to get past them and get away from them. With Ernie you couldn't. Why was that?

A Well, there at the end it really came down to that last pit stop. Goodyear makes the greatest tire in the world and I knew I was going to be racing other Goodyears, but each set we had, we had to adjust a little bit on and we were trying adjust to go the right way there at the end. The car was just a little bit looser than we thought we wanted it to be. These guys did exactly what I asked them to do. Every set is a great set of tires, but they're not always exactly perfect and it was just a little bit different than the last set, and the car just got loose. Even though I jumped out there, I tried to pull away. And Ernie, there isn't anybody can drive harder than Ernie. He was working awfully hard to catch me. When he caught me, I told them, hey, I've got to let him go, guys, because he was really loosening me up, smoking my right rear and burning my tires up. I let him go around me and then I did the same thing to him. And he realized he probably ought to let me go by. So he let me go by and he loosened me up again, just playing. It was like I'd give it to him and he'd give it to me. So I decided, I've got to let him go again, because I can't let him control my race car. He was controlling my race car, so I wanted to get behind him and just wait till the last possible moment that I could. I mean, I waited till five laps to go.

I actually hadn't planned on passing Ernie until three or four laps to go. Then he was going to have to deal with me. We were either going to be in the fence or it's going to be a photo finish to the end, because I was going to race him for everything I had. I know he was wanting to win that thing. I drove in there right on him like I did every lap. I wasn't actually going for the pass with five laps to go. It looked like his car was sliding up, but what it was was his right front was going down.

That's a tough break. I know he's disappointed. The thing is we dominated all day. This isn't like Charlotte. We didn't pop in there and do a two-tire stop. We were beating them on the racetrack just like we wanted to do all day long. Ernie gave us a heck of a fight, no doubt about it. You've got to have everything going your way to win the race these days.

Q Jeff, are you going to take a victory lap through Pittsboro to see that girl that wouldn't give you the time of day when you were in high school?

A (Laughter.) Boy, I think the problem was, I didn't have the time because I was off racing. I wish I could make it to Pittsboro. But I'll tell you, I wish . . . I don't know what I'm going to do.

I know I've got some things planned tomorrow. To all those fans planning on having a fan club meeting like we had scheduled and for all those fans who are going to be down at Tri State or Tri Cities Speedway in Evansville, I hate to break it to 'em, but I'm going to Disney World.

But like I said, I don't know if I'll make it to Pittsboro. I'd love to. I'd love to do it. I heard they put up banners and things and I know they're very proud. I'm proud to say I raced and grew up here in Indiana, and to be here, it's just great.

Q It appears you're on your way to a long and successful NASCAR career. Considering this was in Indiana, at the speedway, the inaugural Brickyard, what would it take to top this?

A Oh, I mean, the topper of them all is the Winston Cup championship. You know, I think it is a little bit out of reach for us this season, but we're a team of the future. And our future is in Winston Cup racing. I know mine is, I know Ray's is and I know Rick Hendrick's is. We want to be a team that is going to win championships down the road and win more races.

I mean, right now we've got to go after our goals, and that's try to go and win more races, lead more laps, do everything it takes to be a championship team. Right now, we're just learning, you know, learning the ropes, learning the racetracks. It's been gradually coming. The cars are getting better, the pit crews are getting better. I feel like our communication is getting better. I feel like my driving is getting better all the time, also.

Q Jeff, when you came down off the fourth turn into the straightaway, could you see the checkered flag out there? Talk about your emotions. What were they the minute you saw that flag wave?

A I was pretty busy the last two or three laps because I was trying . . . like I said, my car was getting looser the longer I ran. I saw Ernie fall out and I came on the radio, you know, "We got 'em, we got 'em." I couldn't believe he was falling off. Then they told me what happened to him. But then here came Brett Bodine. He was pushing that thing awful hard and my car was getting looser and looser and I was trying just to keep the thing, you know, straight and not slip up, not get out of the groove, not get into the way, not do anything like that.

So I was giving up a little bit of time, but I could judge on how fast Brett was closing on me. I felt like we could get there.

When I came off turn four after taking that white flag, I'll tell you, I saw that checkered flag and I came on the radio just screaming and yelling at these guys. And I know they were probably excited, jumping up and down and doing everything. But I took the time out to really tell them the way I felt. And that's when all the emotions came out.

Q For both of you guys. Can you talk about that pit battle when Rusty was in there and you were going after him and Rusty came out first? Can you talk a little bit about that?

A Like I said, I didn't see any of that going on. I was just trying to get out there.

Soon after Jeff Gordon won the Brickyard 400 in 1994, proud residents of Pittsboro proclaimed victory for their hometown hero.   Photo by Scott Sady

59

Brickyard pole sitter Jeff Gordon signs autographs on his way through Gasoline Alley.

Photo by Kristin Enzor

GORDON & GORDON

Dick Mittman, Friday, June 23, 1995

Youthful racers know way around the track.

As the halfway point of the auto racing season arrives, the possibility strongly exists that drivers named Gordon could win championships in the sport's two highest profile series, Indy Car and NASCAR.

Robby Gordon won the last Indy Car race at Detroit and Sunday could overtake PPG Cup points leader Jacques Villeneuve with a good finish in the road course event at Portland, Ore. He trails the most recent Indy 500 winner by only four points, 79-75, heading into the ninth of 17 races.

Over in NASCAR, Jeff Gordon holds third in the Winston Cup standings but is only 12 points behind leader Sterling Marlin and six in arrears to second-place Dale Earnhardt. NASCAR is idle until its traditional midseason 400-mile race on July 1 at Daytona International Speedway, which is No. 16 of the 32-race schedule.

Both Gordons are native Californians but unrelated. Robby was born Jan. 2, 1969, while Jeff came into the world on Aug. 4, 1971.

The odd part about both young, skilled chargers is that each reached the top in his particular series by taking an unusual route. Robby drove off-road vehicles when he was younger, while Jeff, living as a teenager in Pittsboro, Ind., drove USAC open-wheel cars.

Jeff Gordon could at 24 become the youngest champion in NASCAR history. Richard Petty won the first of seven titles in 1964 at age 25. Robby Gordon would become the youngest champion since Mario Andretti won back-to-back crowns in 1965-66.

This is Robby's third full season driving an Indy car, and his maturity shows. He knows now he doesn't have to lead every lap to win. Driving for Derrick Walker, a calm and collected director in the pits, he has learned to pace himself, and this has paid off in two victories and a pair of pole position starts.

"Watching Jeff Gordon, for me, is something else. I see a lot of past history there. I mean, I was always the guy who was called The Kid. I heard that for a long, long time. Now I look at Jeff, and I'm calling him that. But that's OK. I'm still only 36, and I've got a lot of my career in front of me. I'm not jealous of him at all; I'm proud of him. I'm proud that Jeff's the kind of person he is and that what he's accomplished hasn't ruined him in any way."
—Mark Martin

NASCAR driver Jeff Gordon, from Pittsboro, Ind., celebrates his Purolator 500 win as he climbs out of his DuPont Chevrolet in victory lane at Atlanta Motor Speedway in Hampton, Ga., Sunday, March 12, 1995.

Photo by Greg Griffo

"I've heard people say Jeff never had to earn his way. They're crazy. He started racing when he was just a kid, and in go-karts and sprint cars, he was the best. When he started in the Busch series, he'd already won 400 or 500 races. He paid his dues and worked his way up the hardway."

—Buddy Baker

"I think the biggest thing driving for Derrick is that he's good under pressure," Gordon said.

Gordon said the big difference in him from the first year he spent under A. J. Foyt's wing is that he understands the game on the track better.

"What you can do to make things up, you know, as far as pit stops, where the pace car is," he explained. "Maybe I'm a little more alert. And now I've got better equipment under me.

"I'm racing an Indy Car like the NASCAR guys are racing their stock cars. On an oval we want to stay on the lead lap. It's all we really worry about until 50 miles to go. On some of the other tracks, I pace myself and try to save the best for last, because that last 10 laps are definitely the most important 10 laps of the race.

"But you've got to be there. So if you drive 110 percent for a 70-lap race, your odds of finishing are not very good. If you drive 110 percent for 10 laps, your odds are pretty good."

Gordon now has won on an oval (Phoenix) and street-type course this season, so a victory on a pure road course like Portland International Raceway would complete the cycle.

Bill Scherer and grandson Brett Scherer, 6, look at some of the many NASCAR models Scherer has collected since 1990. A cardboard cut-out of Jeff Gordon stands in Scherer's "showroom".

Photo by Rich Miller

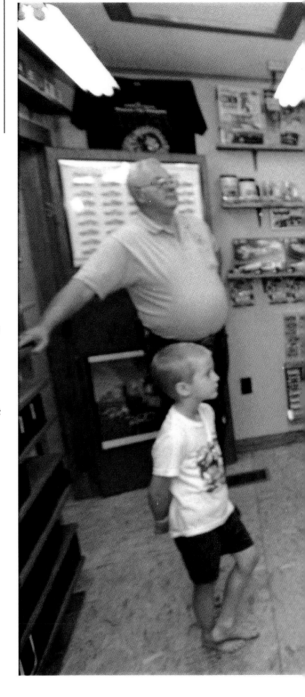

Jeff Gordon spent the earlier part of the week testing at the speedway. He has added another fan in former banker Bob Jayne.

After Gordon won the inaugural Brickyard 400, it occurred to Jayne, a hobby collector of racing memorabilia, that it would be nice to own a yearbook from Tri-West High School from 1989, the year Gordon graduated. He called the school and was told there probably were none left, but a secretary did a little office search and found the last one in a box that was thought to be empty.

Jayne paid $20 for it. A friend suggested he get it autographed and mailed it to Gordon's parents, John and Carol Bickford. He said it would be at least a month before it was returned.

Six months later a large box arrived at Jayne's house. In it was the yearbook autographed inside the front cover.

"He wrote it real big," Jayne said. "The book has his class picture, a picture of him when he was senior homecoming king and a snapshot when he was two or three."

"I tried to get it insured," he said. "One dealer said that whatever he'd give me for it, he could double his money. I wouldn't put a price on it. It's a memory and fun to get it signed."

Photo by Rich Miller

65

Brooke and Jeff
Gordon wave to fans
at the Indianapolis
Motor Speedway in
1995.

Photo by Paul Sancya

Gordon fills role as the favorite in Brickyard 400

Curt Cavin, Sunday, July 30, 1995

Richest race on NASCAR circuit will be worth $4.5 million this time around.

John Andretti has made a couple of trips to Talladega Superspeedway, a place he likens to home. Not Indianapolis, but home as in wife, two kids and a career.

"It's like driving to the airport," he said. "Pick the lane that looks like it might be the fastest and stay with it."

The road has changed and Andretti knows it well. In three days, the most decorated stock car drivers in the United States will arrive at the world's most famous racetrack, Indianapolis Motor Speedway, for many high-speed miles. Instead of hurtling around a 2.66-mile, 33-degree-banked superbowl, the drivers aiming for the second Brickyard 400 title will be negotiating four unique corners and two long and fast straightaways.

Where Talladega rewards horsepower, Indy will honor patience and handling, then horse-power. It's called compromise in finding a setup. A car must glide through the short chutes and power out of the corners. Momentum on the 5/8-mile straightaways will be just as critical since there are few places to pass.

The toughest part might be picking a champion. The top three drivers in Winston Cup points—defending champion Jeff Gordon, Talladega winner Sterling Marlin and seven-time title winner Dale Earnhardt—all drive Chevrolet Monte Carlos, which have won 14 of 18 races this season.

Each seems to have a stronger engine than any of the Ford Thunderbirds, led by team owner Jack Roush and teammates Mark Martin and Ted Musgrave.

However, Ford's Rusty Wallace was as smooth as silk at Indy-like Pocono, which mandates efficiency with chassis handling. His downfall in Pennsylvania was a late-race stop for fuel, enabling fellow Ford driver Dale Jarrett to collect his first victory of the season. Gordon was second.

"The way I look at it, there's room for all of us in this sport. There's room for Dale Earnhardt, Rusty Wallace, for myself, for Dick Trickle, for all of us."

—Mark Martin on Jeff Gordon's success

67

Truth be told, the defending champ must be considered the favorite, having finished first or second in four of the past five races. Two weeks ago at Talladega he was eighth, though he was in the winning draft despite fighting a loose race car and igniting a 12-car accident. The mishap eliminated Hendrick Motorsports teammates Terry Labonte and Ken Schrader, each of whom was capable of winning the race. Both will be contenders this week as well. Jarrett has caught fire in Robert Yates's car, answering his Pocono victory with a second at Talladega.

"I just think it's going to be one heck of a field," Gordon said of the Indy return. "There have been so many guys who have been factors, and this will again be one of the biggest races we've ever run."

The Hulman-George family has enticed the drivers even more, adding an additional $25,000 to each of the finishing positions. The total shows $4.5 million, up $1.3 million from last year, making Indy the richest stop on the 31-race circuit. First place will receive better than $650,000. A dominating run like Gordon had last year could pay in excess of $700,000— that's a whole lot more than Marlin got for winning the Daytona 500 in February ($253,275). Gordon won $613,000 here last year.

In addition, a Brickyard 400 starting position will be worth, in effect, $48,000, minimum. Last year it paid $21,825.

Jeff Gordon celebrates his win atop his car in victory lane at the inaugural Brickyard 400.
Photo by John Gentry

"That's not much less than some of our races pay to win," said Brett Bodine, who ran second to Gordon here last year. "And this purse increase has been distributed throughout the field—not just at the front.

"You'd think Tony George was a car owner himself to figure out a purse structure like that."

The media has spent two weeks trying to gauge the significance of the second Brickyard week, which includes three races at Indianapolis Raceway Park (a Silver Crown race Wednesday, a SuperTruck race Thursday and the annual Kroger 200 Busch Grand National race Friday). The Winston Cup drivers, who begin practice Wednesday afternoon, have said don't bother. Comparisons to last year are fruitless, not to mention inappropriate.

"It's still a big race, there's no doubt about it," said Bobby Labonte, who has won two races this season in Joe Gibbs's Chevy. "It's just not the first anymore.

"With Indy still being Indy, I'm still looking forward to it because the crowd's going to be big and the people are going to be into it. Last year was exciting and I don't see it being any less this time. Nobody has lost anything."

"I agree, there's no way it's going to be as big as the first one," said Gordon. "But from a driver's and a team's standpoint, we all want to win just as much. We'll still be fighting just as hard."

Veteran car owner Bud Moore put it best.

"When last place pays like this one does," he said, "you know everyone is going to be doggin' for Indy."

Brickyard pole sitter Jeff Gordon signs autographs on his way through Gasoline Alley.

Photo by Kristin Enzor

69

Jeff Gordon draws media attention during qualification day for the Brickyard 400 at Indianapolis Motor Speedway.

Photo by Gary Mook

Champ on the defense

Dick Mittman, Wednesday, August 2, 1995

Jeff Gordon seeks a repeat.

Jeff Gordon is back at the Indianapolis Motor Speedway to defend his Brickyard 400 championship. On the track, he is on offense. Off the track, he is on defense.

Gordon returns to Indiana leading the NASCAR point standings by 78 over Sterling Marlin. He has won more races, five, and poles, seven, than any other driver. He has finished in the top five 11 times and in the top 10 13 times in 18 races. He has won $1,667,995 in prize money, and a second consecutive Brickyard victory in his Rick Hendrick DuPont Chevrolet Monte Carlo would jump that to an incredible $2.3 million with 12 races remaining.

That's the upside of Gordon.

The downside is he is being attacked from the flanks by people who are jealous.

The media has begun taking potshots at him because of his purported inaccessibility. He is being derisively referred to by some as "Wonder Boy." Old-timers see him as a Madison Avenue product who can't compare with the rough-tough drivers of their era. Some of the drivers he competes with weekly are tossing out barbed comments. His hometown fans in Pittsboro are being led to believe he has turned his back on them because of a paragraph in a local magazine article.

Through it all, Gordon has tried to keep his affable composure with people tugging at him from all directions. It's not easy.

For instance, at Talladega so many media members wanted interviews, he just didn't have time to grant them individually. So an arrangement was made to bring him to the media room.

There, he answered every question thoughtfully and at length, even some tough ones about his skyrocketing career. He knows there are going to be wrong or tilted stories written about him as his career progresses.

> "I've seen all the great ones—Petty, Pearson, Yarborough, Allison, Waltrip—and none of them accomplished what Gordon has accomplished this early in his career. At this stage he's the best ever."
>
> —Harry Gant

71

Jeff Gordon celebrates with a crew member after winning the first Brickyard 400 at the Indianapolis Motor Speedway in 1994. Gordon is seeking his second victory at IMS.

Photo by John Gentry

"There are now, and I don't let that bother me," he said.

"This one particular incident just concerned me because it's my hometown. When you come from a small town you know how fast things can spread. I wanted to stop it right now. Any other situation I'm going to let roll right off."

One of those pertained to a sign placed on the Gordon transporter that read, "No interviews until after qualifying."

Fellow driver Kyle Petty told *Sports Illustrated*: "I don't think our sport needs that right now. If guys are not as accessible, the whole sport will take a slam. Before, you could never be a smart-aleck, because the other drivers wouldn't let you. Now the sport has grown beyond the grass roots, and drivers are becoming more like football and baseball stars. A lot of drivers are paying lip service to taking care of the fans but not really caring about them."

Ray Evernham, Gordon's crew chief, quickly took blame for the sign. He said it had been up there for two years because the interruptions were distracting from the job at hand. He said it had been removed.

"The sign is not going to be there any more," Gordon assured, "but it's really a situation where when we're practicing we just didn't want somebody to come into the garage when he and I were talking.

"Really, it's a team rule trying to calm things down a little bit while we're practicing. After practice, before practice, that was not a problem. It was the same with autographs. If I'm not working or not in the car, you know, I'm going to give an interview. We took the sign down, and any time we're not in the race car, working under the hood, we're going to try to do as many interviews as we can."

Gordon didn't take public umbrage with Petty's comments.

"Kyle's cool," Gordon said. "He's cool no matter what he says.

"I don't think he meant that in a way to get down on me or the people around me. They're doing a great job, the best they can do to bide my time and help everybody.

"We're just in a situation that's not easy to get around. People are going to make comments, and we're not going to worry about 'em. We're just going to continue to do the best job we can on or off the racetrack."

Gordon thanked the media for agreeing to a mass interview, that it made the race weekend much easier.

"Talk to Ron Miller's office [PR firm]," he said. "They're the guys who get all the calls, especially from the media and for appearances and things like that.

Jeff Gordon and crew chief Ray Evernham (background) check out action around the track.

Indianapolis News Photo

"They don't keep me up on everything because it's so much, but I'll be talking to 'em and they'll say, 'You don't have any idea how many calls are coming into our office.' It means a lot in one way because it's a good problem to have, but there's no way you can take care of every call and every person. It's tough for me and it's tough for them. Nobody likes to say no. There's just certain times when you can't do it all."

Dick Brooks, like Gordon, was a NASCAR Rookie of the Year, but his title dates to 1969. Brooks drove against the likes of Richard Petty and Dale Earnhardt and now owns cars that compete against Gordon's. He was asked to make a comparison between the three.

"Comparing Richard Petty with Jeff Gordon is, they're both race drivers and that's it," he said.

"I've seen Petty sit after a race at Dover some-place, or Darlington, for three hours on a pit wall and sign autographs. And you see Jeff Gordon grab on to his bodyguards and take off down the road.

"A lot of it has to do . . . with the number of people around. The people now are a lot more aggressive. And at that time, they kind of kept a lot of the people away from us that now have access to these guys. And some of these people get pretty aggressive.

"We also were out there trying to sell ourself and trying to make a buck, too. These guys already got their buck made. So there's a lot of difference."

He said there is a much closer comparison between Petty and Earnhardt, because Earnhardt is a racer who didn't have to present himself in the same way to people as The King did. He said Earnhardt raced "good and hard."

Gordon at 21 realized who was the master when he made his full-time Winston Cup debut at the 1993 Daytona 500. He won his 125-mile qualifying race, then in the 500 tucked his car in behind Earnhardt's Chevy and followed everywhere he went on the track for the next three hours.

Now, two years later, it is Earnhardt who is chasing Gordon in the points standings in his bid to become the first eight-time Winston Cup champion.

"At Daytona and Talladega you can learn an awful lot from him," Gordon said.

"How many rookies get to go out there and get in a race car that's capable of even staying on his bumper and racing wheel to wheel with him? I think that's really what was amazing about coming to Hendrick Motorsports, having Ray Evernham there and putting the guys together.

"Here I was with no experience able to have a race car capable of running with these guys. That really helped me more than anything. I didn't have to worry about whether things were going to break. I just had to worry about how fast that race car was and whether I could hold on to it."

Gordon called Earnhardt an incredible driver, one capable of driving in his rear-view mirror more than anyone he had encountered.

"That's pretty tough to do, but that's what it takes to win races," Gordon said. "To work the draft and work the traffic, you've got to know where the guys are at all times before your spotter says clear or inside. You've got to know where they're at before they do. That's probably what I've learned more than anything."

Now that he is running pell-mell toward his first title, Gordon looks to Evernham to help him out in the car. At Talladega, that was particularly true after the incident where Gordon's car touched teammate Ken Schrader's and it went into a wild flip through the infield. Gordon became quite emotional, and Evernham spent the rest of the race calming him down.

"He'll tell you there are times when he feels like he's getting on my nerves," Gordon said. "I need that, and that's what coaches are for.

Fans flock around the Jeff Gordon souvenir trailer during the Brickyard 400 in Indianapolis.

Photo by Kevin O'Neal

"You see football, basketball, baseball, you see coaches. We have a unique situation in NASCAR. We don't call 'em coaches, we call 'em crew chiefs. To me, they're the same thing.

"I've got Ray Evernham and the Rainbow Warriors [crew]. It's not me. It's not him. It's not just one guy on that team. It's everybody that's coming together, and that's what's really making it work now."

Gordon returns to the Brickyard knowing that no matter what happens Saturday, the outcome cannot possibly equal last year's victory in the very first stock car race at the venerable oval on West 16th Street.

"I'm still hoping to win," he said.

"It seems like it can never be what it was. The inaugural race was huge. I hope it can continue to have that magnitude among the media, the sponsors and the fans. I don't know if it will ever have what the inaugural event had.

"I'll always remember that moment, and hopefully, we'll always be remembered for it."

When A. J. Foyt won his first 500-Mile Race in 1961, legend has it White Castle made up his victory banquet after the race.

"Boy, I couldn't handle that," said young Jeff Gordon.

But after he won the inaugural Brickyard 400, he ate pizza.

How he got it delivered to his room was a postrace story in itself.

"We had such a great day and everything just couldn't have gone any more perfect," Gordon said.

"When that race was over we did a lot of interviews. I signed a lot of autographs for fans. There were so many awards given because of all that money and all those sponsors that it took a long time for that day to be over after it was over."

Gordon and his wife, Brooke, returned to the motel and were exhausted. He jumped into some sweats and a T-shirt, flopped out on the bed, and turned on the television just as the delayed telecast was ready to be shown.

"It was kind of like, perfect, what could make this day any better?" he said with a laugh. "You know what we need, we need to order a pizza.

"That turned into the biggest chore I had all day."

First he couldn't find a pizza store that would deliver to the track. When he finally did, they told him it would be 90 minutes.

"I said, what, an hour and 45 minutes? They said, in case you didn't know, there was a big race just happened over there," he said.

Gordon then asked to speak to the manager and, though he didn't want to, told him he was the driver who won that race and if he could get a pizza delivered any quicker it would be much appreciated. The manager called back to the motel to double-check that it was Gordon calling. Once he confirmed it, the pizza was there in 30 minutes.

"That guy got a big tip because of it, too," Gordon said.

Driver Jeff Gordon takes the checkered flag at the end of his qualifying run at the Indianapolis Motor Speedway Thursday, Aug. 3, 1995.

Photo by Steve Noreyko

Success is no accident

Phil Richards, Wednesday, August 2, 1995

It was a setup. With the caution ending, the crowd roaring and the green flag about to wave signaling a restart with one lap to run, Daytona International Speedway's worst seat was its most prominent.

Jeff Gordon occupied it. He was in the lead, with nowhere to go but back.

"You never want to be leading, because those guys are going to split you and go by you and I could see us going back to fifth or sixth," said Ray Evernham, the canny crew chief for Gordon's DuPont Chevrolet. "I didn't know what to do. I thought for sure we were going to get beat."

Drafting is an immutable fact of superspeedway racing, one that seven-time Winston Cup champion Dale Earnhardt has exploited with ruthless efficiency, as 39 superspeedway victories attest. Let the lead car go on the restart. Fall back, hook up with the leading challengers. Then, with the draft pushing-pulling the train at a speed 10 to 12 mph in excess of the lonely leader, make a run he can't possibly hold off.

In a similar situation at Pocono just three weeks earlier, Gordon missed a shift on the restart, over-revved, damaged his engine and fell from first to 16th.

"Every other time I've led there I've gone straight to the back on a restart," said Gordon. "I said to myself, 'You've got to do something different than you've ever done before.'"

As Earnhardt fell back, Gordon sloughed speed with him. The 23-year-old kid from Pittsboro, Ind., pinned NASCAR's dominant driver of the past decade to his bumper. There would be no train. There would be no room. There would be no run. When Gordon finally stood on the gas and let Earnhardt go racing, it was for second place, with Sterling Marlin.

"Pretty awesome stuff. He figured it out," said Evernham. "I saw what he did and I thought, 'The kid's a genius.'

It's a wonder story for Jeff Gordon, Winston Cup's racy "Wonder Boy."

"So as far as Jeff goes, I think it's good for our sport to have young talent. He's an incredibly talented race driver, and he was raised to do this. In fact, when he won his first race at Charlotte, I was almost in tears for him, because I knew that between Jeff and John Bickford and Jeff's mom, their whole lives, forever, had built up to that day. It was just incredible to me, how they got to see that plan succeed."

—Mark Martin

"I don't know what he's got, but if people could answer that there'd be a lot more Michael Jordans and Joe Montanas and Jeff Gordons. I came from the International Race of Champions [IROC] and I got to work with Al [Unser] Jr., Al [Unser] Sr., Michael [Andretti], Mario [Andretti], Earnhardt. They've just got a certain way about them. This kid talks like them. He thinks like them, the mannerisms . . . he's a racer."

That much certainly has been established. Gordon is the Pittsboro prodigy who led 156 of 293 laps at Darlington and 124 of 200 laps at Pocono.

Those are two races he didn't win.

Fact is, Gordon has led at least one lap of all but one of the 18 Winston Cup races this season. He has won five of them and finished in the top five in five others, and he's on a roll. The defending champion will line up Saturday in the Brickyard 400 at the Indianapolis Motor Speedway with two wins and two seconds in his last five starts. He tops the Winston Cup standings with 2,705 points; Marlin is second (2,627), Earnhardt third (2,559).

Hence the sobriquet: "Wonder Boy." It's a nickname Earnhardt enunciates with such glee his smile nearly swallows his trademark moustache.

"He hates it," testified Earnhardt, who has described Gordon as the best young talent in NASCAR history.

"He's a young kid, got a lot of time and a lot of years in the sport. I started 28, 29 years old [in 1979] and now I've won seven championships. He's got the opportunity to win more. He's with the right team."

That would be Hendrick Motorsports, whose other drivers, Terry Labonte and Ken Schrader, rank 11th and 15th in the Winston Cup chase. Gordon has made a career of being in the right place, with the right team, at the right time. It's great stuff for a driver in his third full Winston Cup season, but there is a downside.

A member of a rival team stood in the garage area at Pocono two weeks ago across from the sleek, shiny trailer that transports Gordon's No. 24 car and serves as road shop and office for the DuPont team. He pointed to the sign and proclaimed, "No interviews until after qualifying." He considered Gordon's sudden ascendancy, his burgeoning marketability and his new, perma-pressed, blow-dried appearance.

"That's all we need out here," he snorted, "a preppie Dale Earnhardt."

As Gordon rises, so does the volume.

"I hear the comments. A lot of guys are jealous of him," said Labonte.

"To be blatantly honest with you, nobody likes him," said Kyle Petty. "No, really, that's not it. They're jealous of him. That's what it boils down to. A lot of people say things against him personally in talking and chatting around the garage. People don't think he's paid his dues."

That, it seems, is the real rub. Too much, too soon, too good.

"A lot of other guys have had to struggle a lot more than he ever has, Rusty [Wallace], Dale, myself," Marlin told *The Charlotte Observer*. "We've all been poor enough we haven't had two nickels to rub together. Not Jeff."

Maybe true, maybe not. Gordon is so young, so new and he's been running out front so consistently, many of his peers don't know him.

Defending Brickyard 400 champion Jeff Gordon exits his car after his qualifying record of 172.536 mph at the Indianapolis Motor Speedway. He beat Bobby Hamilton's speed of 172.222 and started first in the field.

Photo by Bob Goshert

Gordon and Brooke Sealey were wed last November, but much of their courtship was conducted in secrecy. NASCAR rules forbid fraternization between drivers and Miss Winston, a pretty face that ornaments Winston Cup functions and a designation that belonged to Sealey in 1993, when Gordon, a rookie, repeatedly showed up at racing gatherings alone.

Earnhardt isn't bashful, but he is curious. He finally popped the question:

"Are you gay?" he asked.

The point is that what people don't know about Jeff Gordon can hurt him. It's a point made by John Bickford, Gordon's stepfather, the man who deftly directed Gordon's racing career from bicycles to the big time.

Most NASCAR drivers and fans don't know Gordon used the move with which he shut down Earnhardt last month at Daytona to beat Danny Smith and Ricky Hood in a sprint car race at Bloomington in 1988. Or that he did it again the next spring to win his first USAC feature, at Florence, Ky. Or that Gordon had watched Earnhardt similarly snooker Al Unser Jr. in an IROC race at Daytona and do it to Gordon himself at Talladega.

"So many people just look at his age, rather than how many years he's raced," said Bickford, who owns an auto parts business. "Sure he's only 23 years old. But this is his 19th racing season.

"To me, to suffer is not paying dues. I think you earn the right to be somewhere and do something by being a creator and an innovator."

Gordon began racing at age four on BMX bicycles. He neither created nor innovated because his mother Carol didn't want him paying those dues. She exercised veto authority after observing an alarming number of young competitors being trundled off to hospitals. So Bickford put Gordon in faster, safer quarter-midget race cars and go-karts.

Gordon was a national quarter-midget champion by the time he was eight and a Hoosier by the time he was 15. The family moved from Vallejo, Calif., to Pittsboro because Jeff could race sprints and midgets at that age in Indiana but not in California.

Home was a house in the country of which the sole furnishings initially consisted of a refrigerator, a washer and dryer and three lawn chairs.

"Few people know Jeff because he doesn't get close to people. But you saw the real Jeff Gordon at New Hampshire. He got bumped off the pole and yet he was the first to congratulate me. That's why he's a friend."
—Ricky Craven, NASCAR driver

"A neighbor came down when we moved in and gave us a big tube of Lebanon bologna," said Bickford. "We were just getting established. We ate fried bologna for breakfast, bologna sandwiches for lunch and bologna and corn for dinner until it was gone."

Gordon didn't have a best friend in high school; he didn't have time. By the time he took driver's education, he had won more than 100 open-wheel races. By the time he turned a wheel in a Winston Cup car, he had won more than 600. He raced two, three, four nights a week. He left graduation ceremonies at Tri-West High School early. There was a race to run.

Gordon won his second quarter-midget national championship in 1981, the USAC midget title in '90 and the USAC Silver Crown championship in '91.

He curled up many nights in the back of a truck. He frequently traded parts for a usable tire or bummed an old one and regrooved it or hustled Hoosier Tire for a freebie.

Gordon was rubbing race cars, not nickels.

"What the heck's paying dues, anyway? Who said you have to pay dues?" asked Petty. "The kid has won in everything he ever drove.

"Jeff comes into the sport and starts winning races right off the bat. What's the difference between that and the NBA player who's making $2.5 million a year and you come right out of college and get $10 million a year? That's a fact. It happens every day in every other sport. But in our sport the guys feel the longer you're out here the more you should be making."

Labonte says that "no one person makes it or breaks it." His point is that whether it's him, Gordon, Earnhardt or Richard Petty, it takes a team, a car, a program. Labonte has won five races driving for Rick Hendrick the past two years after winning zero with Billy Hagan and Richard Jackson the previous four.

Gordon surveys the competition.

Photo by Greg Griffo

That Gordon is in the right place at the right time is no accident. He was Busch Grand National Rookie of the Year in 1991 and won three BGN races and a record 11 poles in 1992. Gordon established those credentials driving a Ford for Bill Davis, so when the decision was made to move up to Winston Cup in 1993, Gordon figured to do it in a Ford, with Davis.

Gordon and Davis went to Chicago early that spring to meet with Target, a prospective sponsor. The meeting adjourned with all parties bullish. All save one. Gordon not only had reservations, he had an alternative. He decided it was time to tell Davis he already had a made a commitment to Hendrick. All that remained was for the contract to be completed and signed. He would drive a Chevrolet. For Hendrick.

Making the decision was difficult. Telling Davis was agony. Gordon remembers that moment as one of the most trying of his life. He took a deep breath. He sighed. He remembered.

"I had to make my choice," he said quietly. "It was very, very difficult."

Michael Kranefuss is now co-owner of the Kranefuss/Haas racing team, whose Ford Thunderbird is driven by John Andretti. At the time Gordon was putting together a Winston Cup package, Kranefuss headed Ford's racing division. He was dining at St. Elmo's in downtown Indianapolis when the phone call came with word of Gordon's decision.

"I was disappointed. In fact, it hurt a lot," said Kranefuss. "But I've got to tell you, I never thought I would do a deal with a 20-year-old kid. It might have been too tough to sell [to the Ford brass]."

What Kranefuss meant was that Ford was unlikely to put Gordon, then 20, in a first-rate ride.

Gordon sensed that. He sensed the sponsorship wasn't solidly committed, that things weren't moving quickly enough. Racers have instincts and Gordon trusted his. He chose Hendrick, where he got an established, successful owner, a sponsor with deep pockets and a strong commitment, a top engine program headed by Randy Dorton, strong research and development and chassis programs directed by Eddie Dickerson and a young but astute crew and crew chief.

No one is doing it better.

"The people who criticized me then, they don't come around now and say I made the right choice," said Gordon. "To me, the jealousy, all that, that's all part of it and it doesn't bother me. I'm not denying the fact I've got great race cars and that there are people all around me making me look good. I've never said I'm the best race car driver in the world. And I won't."

Gordon has had to lease office space. He has hired a secretary to keep track of phone calls and appointments, an accountant to count his money and a banker to handle his merchandise licensing and financial planning.

Country boy has gone corporate. He has fame, fortune and a gilded future but little time and less privacy. He and Brooke recently built a house on Lake Norman, just outside Charlotte, N.C. America comes calling. It comes by car, boat, bike and foot.

"Every construction person, everyone who had anything to do with that house, told all their buddies and they told all their buddies and they told all their buddies," said Gordon. "They don't come up to the front door and knock, but you can't get up in the morning and walk around without wondering who's going to be going by.

"A lot of people think they would love to trade places, but they don't know. There are many more positives about being in this position than there are negatives, but every little thing you do, there's a reaction to it. The toughest part is when you have to say no to somebody for an interview or an appearance or an autograph because you have a priority and you don't have time to sit there and explain why you do what you do."

Bill Elliott knows. Elliott didn't win a race his first seven years in a Winston Cup car. He won 32 over the next seven years, 1983-89, and he was winning fans faster than races. Elliott has been voted Winston Cup's most popular driver nine of the last 11 years. But until he learned to deal with that popularity, it almost crushed him. He hired bodyguards to keep people away.

Jeff Gordon tries to make his way to his garage as he is overtaken by autograph seekers at the Indianapolis Motor Speedway.

Photo by Matt Kryger

"I got spread out by all that stuff and it really hurt my program," said Elliott. "It took me a while to become educated and learn how to deal with fans and media and all that other stuff.

"When you have somebody like a Rick Hendrick or a Ray Evernham who can teach you and show you the ropes and if you get out of line a little bit, spank you around and get you back straight, that makes a lot of difference."

Gordon has grown up over the past few years. He will grow up some more during the next few. There was a time he tended to overdrive his race car on the track and sometimes ran the people around him off it. Evernham, with whom Gordon connects in a way that is both completely natural and a little supernatural, has helped him learn there is a better way.

Like the day at Rockingham last fall when Gordon was horsing a surly race car along the edge, sometimes crossing it. His irritation boiled over.

"When things aren't running good, he's frustrated, I'm frustrated, everybody's frustrated," said Evernham, Gordon's pit boss since his first Busch race. "I was trying to get him to run another lap and he was out there at 150 or 160 mph just trying to save his life and he says something like, 'Well, you might not but I know what's the matter with it.'

"So when he comes in, he says, 'What do you want to do with it?' I said, 'I don't know. You know what's the matter with it. Put it up on a jack stand and fix it.'"

Evernham walked away. Ten minutes later, Gordon sought him out and apologized. "You can't talk to people like that," Evernham admonished his young driver.

It's interesting that Gordon's first Winston Cup race, Atlanta in 1992, was Richard Petty's last. It's a fact that Gordon has won seven Winston Cup races, 193 fewer than Richard Petty, and zero Winston Cup championships, seven fewer than Earnhardt. Jeff Gordon is no Richard Petty or Dale Earnhardt, but, like them, he seems able to see the line and drive it.

They're not calling anyone else out there "Wonder Boy."

Jeff Gordon stands in the pits during qualifications for the Brickyard 400 at Indianapolis Motor Speedway. Photo by Gary Mook

Jeff Gordon takes an early lead in the Brickyard 400.

Photo by Steven Noreyko

Gordon left wondering what went wrong this time

Bill Benner, Sunday, August 6, 1995

Jeff Gordon was Wonder Boy once again Saturday at the Indianapolis Motor Speedway.

Only this time, it meant wondering where the handling went in his No. 24 DuPont Monte Carlo.

Awakened from a nap for the rain-delayed start of the second Brickyard 400, the pole sitter and defending champ threatened to put the rest of the field to sleep, charging to a three-second lead 30 laps into the run and the first round of pit stops.

And while the Speedway oval may be a relatively level track, for Gordon it was all downhill from there. The pride of Pittsboro eventually finished sixth.

Running out front was one thing. But as soon as Gordon encountered traffic, he had to come to grips with the reality that the front of his car didn't have any grip.

"The worst part was that we couldn't get close to anybody," said the 24-year-old. "The front end would just slide right out. When we were leading, we were in command. But as soon as we got behind, the car started going away. The harder I drove it into the corner, the worse it was. Even a lapped car, I had to get a run on them. Even with cars a lot slower, I couldn't get around them, and that killed us a couple of times."

Gordon's frustration came through loud and clear in radio transmissions to crew chief Ray Evernham.

"This car's terrible!" he exclaimed at one point.

"Worst car I've had since Daytona," he said later.

At the end of the race, however, Gordon was diplomatic.

"Ray's very good at guessing what to start the race with and we started with a good setup," he said. "But the track changed and the tires were a little different with certain sets. I think

> "I always watch the Truck races and the Busch races and Cup races from the past. I love races. A lot of times I watch other types of racing like motorcycle racing or Formula One—things like that. But when I'm at a racetrack and I'm in my motor coach and the Busch race or the Truck race is on, I'm definitely going to watch it."
>
> —Jeff Gordon

Jeff Gordon, right front, takes off at the start of the 1995 Brickyard 400, won by Dale Earnhardt. Gordon, the pole sitter, finished sixth at the Indianapolis Motor Speedway.

Photo by Mike Fender

we just adjusted the wrong way. I might have fed the wrong information back to Ray and we got off somewhere. We came back and got it close, but we couldn't find it again there at the end."

The youngster also realizes there's not much sense in rocking the boat that's leading the flotilla.

Gordon's sixth-place finish enabled him to stay atop the Winston Cup point standings.

Better still, it earned him a $100,000 bonus from series sponsor R. J. Reynolds for being the points leader after the series' 19th race. He already earned a similar bonus for leading after nine races.

That swelled Gordon's take for the week even more. The combination of the bonus, winning the pole on Thursday and leading 35 laps on Saturday left him with a sweet $299,200 for the week—a total surpassed only by winner Dale Earnhardt.

"We're a strong team right now and we just don't want to get ourselves down," Gordon said. "This is a big race and we're a little disappointed, and we surely would have liked to win it again because we know how special it is to be on that podium where Earnhardt's at right now.

"We've just got to keep doing what we're doing. A sixth here and an eighth at Talladega [the previous race] are not the best finishes, but they're still top 10 and that's very important.

"Again, we go out to win and when we don't win we're going to be disappointed. And hopefully, I'll be in the lead at the right time at the end of the season."

Indeed, the kid's future is so bright he has to wear shades. And he had those cool oval numbers on even as he stepped into the gathering dusk Saturday evening.

His fans were waiting, shouting his name and singing his praises.

A year ago, he left the Speedway a winner. Saturday night, even in defeat, he departed a champion and a racer to be reckoned with each and every week.

"He's been doing great things and is a great racer," said Earnhardt. "He deserves the due he's gotten."

Gordon returned the praise.

"[Dale's] a good guy, a heck of a competitor and one great name for me to be next to as a winner of this race."

Jeff Gordon seeks shelter under an umbrella during driver introductions before the start of the 1995 Brickyard 400, which was rain-delayed.

Photo by Mike Fender

Winston Cup champion Jeff Gordon is swarmed by fans and members of the media after winning the championship during the NAPA 500 at Atlanta Motor Speedway in Hampton, Ga., Sunday, Nov. 12, 1995.

Photo by Greg Griffo

Western Diversified
510 Lake Cook Rd.
Deerfield, IL 60015

The second fastest service in the business!

20132

August, 1 1996

Pay to the
order of __Pole Winning Crew Chief__ | $ 5,000.00

Five Thousand and 00/100's ----------- Dollars

For Brickyard 400

0712156113   456100 189   88510 20132

Lloyd Gearhart

Jeff Gordon's crew chief Ray Evernham, carrying the Pole Crew Chief check, stops to sign an autograph for a fan Friday, Aug. 2, 1996. The day before, Gordon won his second straight Brickyard pole. Driving a record speed of 176.419 mph, he knocked Mark Martin from the top spot.

Photo by Bob Goshert

Heart & desire bring Gordon another pole

Curt Cavin, Friday, August 2, 1996

Former Hoosier establishes track record after posting 27th best time in previous day's practice.

Jeff Gordon became the 16th driver in Indianapolis Motor Speedway history to twice earn the pole position. Indy cars have raced here 80 years. Gordon accomplished this feat in just three stock car trips.

This one came as a surprise.

In qualifying for the third Brickyard 400, the soon-to-be 25-year-old ran nearly a half-second better than his all-time best. The lap of 51.015 seconds (176.419 mph) also was 0.144 faster than the closest of his 47 challengers.

After exiting turn one of his one-lap effort, Gordon looked into the massive grandstands to see hands waving. A thought traveled through his mind: "Good enough? No way."

By the backstretch, he realized. On pit road the scoring pylon with his number on top gave him a warm, home-cooked feeling.

"If you have a lot of heart and desire, it makes things come together," the former Hoosier said. "That's what this team has and I drove my heart out. It was a good lap . . . but I really didn't think we were capable of running those speeds.

"It was all we had to offer."

Gordon qualified third for the inaugural Brickyard in 1994, then came back to win the race and begin his championship form. Last year, he set a track record in earning his first Indy pole.

There was a primary difference between the pole-winning years, however. Last year, he hung his DuPont-sponsored Chevrolet on the line to the point where he was out of control in the fourth turn. His rear swung wide and he nearly crashed. In dirt-track fashion, he captured it and motored on.

"He's a good guy and I really think people are jealous of him a little bit because he's so successful, he's so young and he's so good and it's really not fair. I've seen him pull out on pit road and I'll pull out behind him and people will be shaking their fist at him and making obscene gestures to him and I'm like, 'Man, here's a guy that doesn't ever say anything bad, he doesn't ever do anything bad.' I mean he's just a good guy and he runs good and wins races and these people are just jealous of him because he is that good."

—Terry Labonte, Hendrick Motorsports teammate

Jeff Gordon greets a hometown crowd after winning the pole during qualifying for the 1996 Brickyard 400. Gordon's qualifying time was 176.415 mph.

Photo by Susan Plageman

Thursday's ride was perfect. He raced through the first and second turns in record pace and sailed smoothly through turn three, his favorite. Turn four was the last hurdle.

It did not prove to be the quickest run through the last corner—Greg Sacks and Dale Jarrett ran 169 mph to Gordon's 167—but it was good enough. The Chevy was pointed south and the Hendrick-powered V8 engine was effectively aggressive.

"The pressure was on," said Gordon, his lap better than Mark Martin's (51.159 seconds, 175.922 mph). "I kept thinking about turn four, 'I know it's going to get loose, don't let it get loose like last year.' I didn't know if I could save it again."

An estimated 40,000 spectators watched the first day of qualifying, which locked in the top 25 starters for Saturday's 160-lap race. Positions 26 through 38 will be determined with second-round qualifying today. NASCAR will use its formula to fill the rest of the field, which most likely will grid with 42 drivers.

Third-day practice begins at 10 this morning and runs for 90 minutes. Following qualifications there will be a one-hour final practice. Gates open at 7 a.m.

Gordon's run Thursday came 43rd in the order and with less anticipation than in the previous two years of the event. The defending Winston Cup champion was 27th in practice Wednesday, and though he improved four-tenths of a second with a fresh engine, he was only 17th in Thursday morning's two-hour session.

In fact, Gordon was the fifth best Chevy in a speed chase dominated by Fords. Bobby Hillin Jr. (Ford) and Joe Nemechek (Chevy) shared the morning's top practice lap at 51.142 seconds, the best to date.

"I thought I was going to have to get every little bit out of the car just to get in the top 10," Gordon said. "It's not that we were sandbagging, it's that we were struggling."

Gordon said he and crew chief Ray Evernham began clicking in their communications near the end of the Thursday practice and were dialed in for qualifications. Still, it was a one-lap effort that had to be perfect. Gordon nailed it and gained another four-tenths to pass the field.

He said his RPMs down the backstretch were as good as he'd seen "in a while." USAC's timing and scoring system clocked him at a field-high 185 mph. Gordon was also dynamite in the second corner, which he had predicted would be critical to running well.

Jeff Gordon leaves a trail of fire after hitting the wall coming out of turn four during the 1996 Brickyard 400. The bump apparently knocked loose the race car's fuel pump. After starting in the pole position, Gordon finished 37th after completing only 40 laps.

Photo by Marty Sullivan

"Everyone can drive it deep into the corner," he said, "but it's hard to get off [turns two and four]. If I could have one thing, that's what I'd want."

Martin appeared to be pole worthy until Gordon's late heroics. He will start second, knocking off track records posted earlier in the day by Dick Trickle, Jimmy Spencer, Rick Mast and Ken Schrader, respectively.

By the time the 48 cars qualified, Trickle had been pushed to 25th, the last of the guaranteed positions. His Ford was one of the 14 locked in with Chevy grabbing eight and Pontiac three.

John Andretti claimed the 26th spot, the best of the non-qualifieds.

There were no accidents in the first day of qualifying, except for Dale Jarrett's slapping of the turn four wall. He was not injured and managed to finish as the 24th quickest (174.260 mph).

The day's other significant accomplishment belonged to Dale Earnhardt, the seven-time series champion who, despite a broken collarbone and sternum, qualified 12th. Earnhardt did not practice Wednesday and intends to give up his seat shortly after receiving the green flag Saturday.

Mike Skinner will relieve him.

"I'm a little tender," Earnhardt said, "and I'm still a little sore. The car is a lot faster than I ran it."

Jeff Gordon celebrates on the roof of his car after his Brickyard 400 victory at the Indianapolis Motor Speedway on Aug.1, 1998. With the victory, Gordon became the race's first two-time champion. Photo by Joe Vitti

Jeff and Brooke Gordon pull the ribbon to unveil a Jeff Gordon Boulevard sign on the stage at Dr. Malcolm Scamahorn Park in Pittsboro, Ind. The NASCAR driver was on hand to absorb the adulation of his fans and ride in a Brickyard 400 Z-28 Camaro pace car.

Photo by Joe Vitti

Gordon owns the road

Curt Cavin, Friday, August 6, 1999

Two-time champ sets record in qualifying.

They say Jeff Gordon is a formidable competitor. He showed that Thursday in record time.

Gordon won the pole for Saturday's Brickyard 400 at the Indianapolis Motor Speedway by running 179.612 mph (50.108 seconds)—the fastest NASCAR time ever on the track.

"He's a better driver than at least most of us, if not all of us," said rival Mark Martin. "And he's driving a better car than most of us, if not all of us.

"When you put that together, it's a hard combination to beat."

Throw in the location of Thursday's time trials—the historic track is Gordon's favorite—and the odds were heavily in the onetime Hoosier's favor.

The former Pittsboro, Ind., resident won the Brickyard 400 pole in 1995 and 1996. He won the race in 1994 and '98.

"This is a place that always feels right to me," said Gordon, who turned 28 on Wednesday and was honored by having part of a road named for him in Pittsboro. "I can't explain it. I just seem to run well here and obviously I've had pretty good cars here."

Before a crowd estimated at 50,000, Gordon said he misjudged Thursday's weather conditions. The bright sun and strong headwind caused him to miss his preferred line through the first turn.

When he completed the one-lap dash around the 2.5-mile oval, he thought his DuPont Chevrolet would be a tick off the pole pace.

Then he saw his speed. It was better than his morning practice run (178.720).

"From living with him for five years, everyone has their downfalls, but Jeff is a really neat individual. It's a shame he's become so popular and people want to take shots at him, because he's really a great guy."

—Andy Graves, Chip Ganassi Racing team manager

NASCAR driver Jeff Gordon signs autographs for his fans in Dr. Malcolm Scamahorn Park in Pittsboro. Jeff was at a ceremony to rename Hendricks County Road 275 East "Jeff Gordon Boulevard."

Photo by Joe Vitti

It also eclipsed Ernie Irvan's record of 179.394 mph, set last year in qualifying.

"I was not expecting to sit on the pole because I slipped [in the first turn]," Gordon said. "I thought that if someone didn't slip, they had it."

No one took it away, giving Gordon his seventh pole of the season and his 30th in seven seasons.

Bobby Labonte was the quickest in the morning practice session (179.119 mph), but he and the Interstate Batteries Pontiac challenged the Speedway about an hour later than Gordon, when the track was warmer. With a lap of 178.642 mph, Labonte settled for the seventh starting spot in the sixth Brickyard 400.

Series points leader Dale Jarrett also figured to be a pole contender, but he bobbled in the first turn, too, and slipped to fourth in the Quality Care Ford (178.859).

"We missed it just a little bit," Jarrett said. "The track was a little slicker than it was [in the morning practice]."

David Green upstaged the usual Winston Cup hotshots with a lap of 178.902 mph, good for a career-best third starting spot. It was the same Kodiak Chevrolet that he failed to qualify with in last month's race at Loudon, N.H.

Customers at the Dairyland store on East Main Street in Plainfield, Ind., have the opportunity to purchase their soft drinks from the vending machines featuring their favorite NASCAR drivers. From left are former Pittsboro resident Jeff Gordon, Dale Earnhardt and son Dale Jr., Columbus, Ind., native Tony Stewart and Dale Jarrett.
Photo by Joe Vitti

Fortieth in car owner points, Green's team likely needed to qualify in the top 36 to make the race. The final seven starting positions in the 43-car field are reserved for the non-qualified teams highest in the standings.

"I knew if I didn't try too hard, we would have a chance of getting in the top 10," Green said. "We needed to make this race. I promise I'll sleep good tonight."

Michael Waltrip was fifth in the Philips Chevrolet, with Mike Skinner sixth in the Lowe's Chevrolet.

Martin grabbed the outside pole, his second in a row, with a lap of 178.941 mph. The driver of the Valvoline Ford seemed disappointed by his performance.

"We look at the pole as a competition within the competition," Martin said. "Everybody wants to win everything."

Martin's day included contact with Rusty Wallace's car on a congested pit road during the late-afternoon practice. Wallace pulled out in front of him off the Gasoline Alley access road. Wallace's car suffered the most damage, all on the right front fender.

Both cars will be repaired.

"Mark didn't expect me to be coming out, and I didn't expect him to be coming down pit road," said Wallace, driver of the Miller Lite Ford. "It was nobody's fault."

Derrike Cope was the only Winston Cup driver to make wall contact. He bounced off the concrete during his qualifying run. It dropped him and the Jimmy Dean Pontiac to 30th.

Cope and 28 other drivers will compete for 18 positions in second-round qualifying today. Teams have the option of standing on their Thursday efforts or withdrawing for a second try. Those decisions will be made this morning. Among those uncertain for the race: Ricky Craven (26th), Wally Dallenbach Jr. (27th), Darrell Waltrip (32nd), Irvan (46th) and Bobby Hamilton (53rd). Waltrip has to make the top 36—he has exhausted his allotment of provisional starting tickets.

Today's action includes the last of this season's four International Race of Champions events. Dale Earnhardt has won the first three and can wrap up the title by finishing eighth or better.

Jeff Gordon is introduced to the crowd before the Brickyard 400 on Aug. 5, 2000.

Photo by Kerry Keating

Everyone enters the pit area (Gordon in damaged light blue car halfway down pit road) during a yellow flag following a John Andretti crash on lap 43, Saturday afternoon, Aug. 5, 2000, at the Indianapolis Motor Speedway during the seventh Brickyard 400.

Photo by Kelly Wilkinson

Jeff Gordon looks at the track before the final practice session for the 2001 Daytona 500, Feb. 17.

Photo Greg Griffo

Rivalry of respect

Curt Cavin, Sunday, March 11, 2001

Jeff Gordon, Dale Earnhardt were linked by excellence, and young star will miss fire of Intimidator.

Jeff Gordon stands just a shade taller than 5'7", short even by NASCAR's driver standards. He never considered it an issue.

His measuring stick was Dale Earnhardt.

That explains why when Earnhardt, the seven-time Winston Cup champion, died in a last-lap accident in the Daytona 500 last month, a part of Gordon died, too. He and Earnhardt were not particularly close as friends off the track—never "fishing buddies," as Gordon terms it—but they were linked by their competitiveness.

As a rookie in 1993, Gordon used Earnhardt to gain strength in the eyes of the sport's loyal fans. Gordon challenged Earnhardt whenever he could, and he was most successful at Daytona (Fla.) International Speedway, a track where Earnhardt excelled the most.

Gordon was 21 years old the first time he raced Earnhardt at Daytona. He studied every move Earnhardt made and rode in the black car's tracks so long, his rainbow-colored car wore a thin layer of Earnhardt's black Goodyear tire rubber.

Gordon won the Twin 125 qualifying race that week. He lost a chance to win the 500 because he followed Earnhardt's race-leading line and they were passed by a three-car draft in the third turn of the last lap. Earnhardt fought back to finish second (behind Dale Jarrett); Gordon settled for fifth.

"I learned a hard lesson," Gordon said after the race.

When Gordon got to the International Race of Champions series in 1995, he still followed Earnhardt's lead. Where Earnhardt drove, Gordon followed. He raced The Intimidator as hard as anyone in stock car racing dared to do.

To everyone's surprise, Earnhardt loved it.

"Who's the best ever? I think that's impossible to tell. But Gordon is awfully good, I can tell you that."
—Richard Petty

111

Jeff Gordon, top, gives Dale Earnhardt a thumbs up after Earnhardt won the 1995 Brickyard 400 at the Indianapolis Motor Speedway. Gordon was the pole sitter but finished sixth in the race. Gordon won the 1994 race.   Photo by Mike Fender

"We all have people we look up to, people we respect and learn from when it's early in our careers," Earnhardt once said. "For me, it was great to learn from guys such as David Pearson, Bobby Allison and Richard Petty.

"When Gordon came along, if he wanted to talk to me and pick my brain I was glad to help him."

Their unique bond—Southern champion and California-born Midwesterner—spilled into the grandstands. The fans either loved Earnhardt (and therefore hated Gordon) or hated Earnhardt (and adored the innocent-looking Gordon). A rivalry developed.

Gordon reaped the rewards: TV coverage, souvenir sales and success.

"He became the guy who could challenge Dale," said Ray Evernham, Gordon's crew chief at Hendrick Motorsports at the time.

Gordon's emergence

Gordon won the inaugural Brickyard 400 at the Indianapolis Motor Speedway in 1994, a year ahead of Earnhardt. Gordon even beat his rival to the checkered flag in the Daytona 500, winning the sport's Super Bowl in 1997. Earnhardt ended his 20-year drought the next year.

He took a 2-1 Indy lead over Earnhardt in 1998. He also won a second Daytona 500.

Earnhardt always needled Gordon. When Gordon won the 1999 Daytona 500, Earnhardt put a tire mark on his car during the victory lap, for everyone to remember him by.

In 1995, when Gordon was shaping up as a championship contender, Earnhardt said NASCAR officials would have to adjust their awards banquet if Gordon, then 23, won. He said Gordon wouldn't be old enough to drink the victory champagne at the Waldorf-Astoria Hotel in New York. Earnhardt suggested Gordon swig on milk.

It became something of a joke in the garage area, and Gordon played the part, right up to the point where he received the championship trophy and the glass with which to toast it.

As Earnhardt had suggested, Gordon received milk. The young champion never broke stride, toasting Earnhardt, whose smile was as vast as a big brother's. The mutual respect was obvious.

"Dale was a compassionate person who would razz you and have fun, but yet, he was The Intimidator," Gordon said last month at North Carolina Speedway, after Earnhardt's death. "There was no doubt he lived up to that name."

Jeff Gordon looks over his head-and-neck restraint before climbing into the No. 24 Chevy during the second day of testing at Indianapolis Motor Speedway, Tuesday, July 17, 2001.

Photo by Greg Griffo

Gordon paused to tell his favorite Earnhardt story, one that came with his first invitation to the IROC series. Gordon was as green as he could be with the 12-driver all-star series, so he figured he should, like always, run with and learn from Earnhardt.

Gordon was driving beside Ken Schrader in a practice session at Daytona when Earnhardt came roaring up from behind.

"Dale took it three-wide," Gordon said. "I looked over at Schrader and he was looking straight ahead [in a closed-faced helmet], very focused.

"Then I looked over at Dale and he was just beaming [out his open-faced helmet] with a great big smile. He was just having a ball out there. That's just the way he was.

"He knew he wasn't going to lift [off the throttle]; I was going to have to lift, and sure enough, I did. When we came back in [the pits], I said it was unbelievable to me that a guy that had never run in IROC and had only been in Winston Cup for only one year had to be the bigger man to let off the gas."

For all of Earnhardt's intimidation, he was the driver who could most freely walk into the NASCAR trailer and discuss—or influence—the shapers of the rules. He also could alter the tone of a drivers' meeting with a few pointed words.

His presence will be missed. Every driver knows a replacement will be needed.

While fellow driver Steve Park believes no one can fill Earnhardt's shoes, he thinks Gordon, a three-time series champion, is one of the few who can step into a major leadership role.

"Jeff Gordon is a young, talented guy that has taken a different approach to helping NASCAR grow, and it's guys like him, and some of the younger guys behind him, who can change the face of NASCAR over the next 10 years."

Gordon said Earnhardt had suggested he take a larger role before the tragedy.

"He'd voice his opinion and he encouraged me to go up [to the NASCAR trailer] and just sit up there and talk," Gordon said. "I don't know if he knew or felt like that was his responsibility, but it was just a part of being a champion. You have to get comfortable spending time in that truck or picking up the phone and calling people."

For Gordon, the link to Earnhardt is rooted in dominance. They combined to win seven of the 10 Winston Cup titles in the 1990s.

Gordon will miss Earnhardt.

"I don't know if I ever expected something like this in my whole career," Gordon said. "I never thought [Earnhardt] would ever even quit, you know.

"I just thought I'd always be racing Dale Earnhardt and that black No. 3 car."

The rookies, with the exception of fifth-place Kurt Busch, had typical rookie finishes.

The Robert Yates duo of Dale Jarrett and Ricky Rudd weren't able to show off their vaunted horsepower.

And the Dodges, which many feared might run away and hide because of aerodynamic help extended them last week by NASCAR, wound up spread throughout the field, as usual.

In fact, the first four finishers drove four makes of cars—Gordon (Chevrolet), Sterling Marlin (Dodge), Johnny Benson (Pontiac) and Rusty Wallace (Ford).

Also put to rest was the notion that stock cars can't pass at Indianapolis Motor Speedway. The race didn't exactly remind anyone of Bristol, Tenn., on a Saturday night, but neither was it 42 cars following the leader.

The decisive pass came on a restart on the 136th of 160 laps. It came after the day's seventh and final caution, during which Gordon's crew chief, Robbie Loomis, decided to go with just a two-tire change to get his driver closer to the front.

"When you get Jeff Gordon towards the front, it's going to be a beautiful sight," Loomis said.

Not to Marlin, who chose to stay on the track and take the lead. Gordon was first out of the pits and immediately began sizing up Marlin.

When the green flag fell, Gordon went to the inside and zipped past, never to be caught.

"For some reason with our car, we have

Jeff G
photo
Motor
line.

Dee Durand of Kearney, Neb., shows her support for her favorite driver, Jeff Gordon, at the Indianapolis Motor Speedway. When asked why she enjoys NASCAR, she said, "I love that noise...that thunder, the smell of the tires, the fuel...the speed!"   Photo by Rich Miller

Jeff Gordon kisses the Brickyard 400 trophy after winning the race at the Indianapolis Motor Speedway, Sunday Aug. 5, 2001. Gordon became the first three-time winner of the Brickyard 400.

Photo by Matt Kryger

Jeff Gordon does a burnout at the start/finish line after winning the Brickyard 400 at the Indianapolis Motor Speedway.

Photo by Matt Kryger

a lot of trouble on restarts," Marlin said. "It just wouldn't go."

Marlin doggedly hung on, but Gordon, with his car finally out of traffic and near-perfect in clean air, was in the clear.

"I wanted to put more pressure on him and make him make a mistake," Marlin said, "but I just couldn't get close enough."

In the process of widening his gap on Marlin, Gordon also moved farther ahead in the Winston Cup points standings as his two closest pursuers, Jarrett and Rudd, finished 12th and 39th, respectively.

Other than Gordon, the Indiana contingent had a tough day. Tony Stewart brushed the wall, limped home 17th and went away mad. Rookie Ryan Newman led briefly before having a close encounter with the wall and finishing 31st.

"I had a slight bit of help from Jimmy [Spencer]," Newman said of his incident, "but I can't blame it all on him."

Gordon's previous victories in the Brickyard came in 1994 and '98. Team owner Rick

Hendrick was undergoing cancer treatments for the last one and was not in attendance.

"I've seen people kiss those bricks all my life," Hendrick said. "I never dreamed I'd get to come to [IMS], let alone have a car in the race and win."

But then, he couldn't have dreamed he would have the opportunity to hire a driver like Jeff Gordon, who already has 56 wins with the prime of his career still to come.

"It's been such a flash. It's gone by so fast," Gordon said of the last decade. "I have done some things that I could never have imagined.

"I just hope the next 10 years are as good as the last 10."

Brickyard 400 champion Jeff Gordon high-fives fans following the victory podium photos at the Indianapolis Motor Speedway.

Photo by Rich Miller

121

Jeff Gordon leads the pack with three laps to go en route to his third victory in the Brickyard 400 at Indianapolis Motor Speedway.

Photo by Steve Healey

2001 Brickyard 400 winner Jeff Gordon acknowledges the crowd as he celebrates in victory lane.
Photo by Steve Healey

Gordon
makes it 3

Steve Ballard, Monday, August 6, 2001

Two tires on late pit stop prove to be decisive move.

The fans who cheer Jeff Gordon the loudest were able to cheer him the longest on Sunday at the Indianapolis Motor Speedway.

The homegrown talent won the hometown race for a record third time, beating Sterling Marlin to the checkered flag in the eighth running of the Brickyard 400.

Gordon clearly was the crowd favorite among the more than 300,000 in attendance, and he didn't disappoint. The three-time NASCAR Winston Cup champion came from 27th on the grid—the farthest back a Brickyard winner has started—to record his 56th career victory one day after his 30th birthday.

While no longer the target of boos everywhere he goes, neither is Gordon a crowd favorite anywhere other than Indiana.

"To have all these people cheering us on like that, I got tears in my eyes in the car," Gordon said. "I love Indianapolis."

The Hendrick Motorsports team's pit strategy proved decisive. Crew chief Robbie Loomis ordered up two tires instead of four during a late stop to save time and gain track position. Gordon then zipped past Marlin on a restart and led the final 25 laps around the 2.5-mile track.

2001 Brickyard 400 winner Jeff Gordon's pit crew celebrates the win moments after Gordon crosses the finish line.

Photo by Steve Healey

The DuPont Chevrolet pit crew celebrates after driver Jeff Gordon won his third NASCAR Brickyard 400 Sunday, Aug. 5 at the Indianapolis Motor Speedway. He passed Sterling Marlin on a restart to take the lead and held it to the end of the race.　　Photo by Joe Vitti

Gordon won the inaugural Brickyard 400 in 1994. His '98 victory propelled him to his third series championship, and he leaves town this time with a commanding lead in the Winston Cup standings.

Johnny Benson, Rusty Wallace and rookie Kurt Busch completed the top five finishers. Wallace started 37th and Busch 34th, joining Gordon to belie the notion that the Brickyard is a no-passing zone.

"I think I got a few new gray hairs today," Gordon said. "To be able to come from 27th and win, I think that's an indication our team can do just about anything."

Jeff Gordon takes the checkered flag as he crosses the yard of bricks to win the Brickyard 400 at the Indianapolis Motor Speedway. Gordon became the first three-time winner of the Brickyard 400.

Photo by Matt Kryger

Jeff Gordon takes the lead from Kevin Harvick in lap 110 of the 2001 Brickyard 400 at Indianapolis Motor Speedway.

Photo by Chris Preovolos

Gordon: Better than Petty, Earnhardt?

C. Jemal Horton, Tuesday, August 7, 2001

It all was supposed to end when Ray Evernham walked away from Jeff Gordon in 1999.

The dominance.

The smiling.

Those victories, man.

And much of it did slow down in 2000. Gordon-haters could grin a symbolic sigh of relief, because virtually all of NASCAR's hallowed drivers and records might be safe, now that the Boy Wonder no longer had Evernham, his old crew chief, his key to success.

That is part of what made Gordon's fourth victory of this Winston Cup season amazing.

The Brickyard 400 victory Sunday at Indianapolis Motor Speedway was merely a small step toward a glorious position Gordon might be taking.

Just maybe, he is the greatest NASCAR driver ever.

Right now. At 30 years old.

Once again, Gordon is the most dominating driver in his sport at the moment. He is that even without Evernham, now a team owner who works with Dodges instead of Gordon's recognizable DuPont Chevy.

The key to Gordon's success is Gordon himself.

Of course, racing is the epitome of a team sport, but the driver has to get it done.

> "I'll tell you, I get to speak a lot publicly, and I tell everybody right up front they need to meet Jeff Gordon because he's just a super, super nice guy. He's doing what he gets paid to do, and he's doing a great job at it. You know, a lot of people don't like Jeff, but Jeff's a winner and he's awesome. He's really a role model for a lot of people."
> —"Chocolate" Myers, Richard Childress Racing's No. 29 gasman

129

Billy Britton holds his wife Billie Britton up in the air as she tries to see Jeff Gordon in the victory circle after DuPont Chevrolet driver Jeff Gordon won the NASCAR Brickyard 400 at Indianapolis Motor Speedway, Sunday, Aug. 5, 2001. The Brittons, from Lafayette, Ind., are big Jeff Gordon fans.

Photo by Joe Vitti

It is hard to say if Gordon is the best ever for sure, because it is so hard to compare athletes from different eras. Auto racing may be an even rarer case, because there are so many rules changes, so many track adjustments, so many technological advances every time you turn around. Especially in NASCAR.

What would Richard Petty, a man some consider the greatest driver ever, do in 2001 with all the new advantages at his disposal? What would the late Dale Earnhardt, the only other driver considered the greatest ever, be doing to racetracks if he, too, were 30?

They'd both be amazing. But it's hard to believe they'd be topping Gordon.

After the Brickyard 400 victory Sunday, many people were openly wondering if Gordon is the "Michael Jordan of NASCAR."

Perhaps he is. It is hard to argue against it.

Gordon already has three Winston Cup points championships and should win his fourth this season. He has 56 career wins. He isn't at the top of many lists now. But he will be.

Petty and Earnhardt each had seven points titles. That's impressive. But Petty raced 35 years and Earnhardt 26. Gordon is not far behind them, and he's only in his ninth full season on the circuit.

Petty has 200 career victories, more than any other driver. But again, so many things change in NASCAR. When Petty raced, there often were weeks in which there was more than one race.

Jeff Gordon signs autographs and talks with fans in the garage as the team readies the car for final inspection before the 2001 Daytona 500. Photo by Greg Griffo

A final comparison: Petty had 1,185 starts, which means he won about 17 percent of the time. Earnhardt had 673 starts and 76 career victories, winning about 11 percent of the time. Gordon has 278 starts, which means he's won 20 percent of the time. In today's racing, that's amazing.

So, yeah, it seems wild to entertain it, but Gordon could make an argument for being the greatest ever.

"Sometimes, it is hard to believe that I've done some of the things that I've done," Gordon said.

Now Gordon is making his new crew chief look good. Robbie Loomis came over from Petty Enterprises. He was one of the first to dub Gordon "Michael Jordan."

And suddenly, Loomis is the next Ray Evernham. That's no shabby comparison.

"This team is the greatest race team," Loomis said. "And so is that driver."

Minister Dale Beaver with Motor Racing Outreach shares a laugh with driver Jeff Gordon as he makes his rounds through the garage area. "I enjoy the relationships I have with the drivers and I enjoy keeping them faithful," said Beaver. "I am here for a reason far different than anyone else out here. I do what I can to help everybody do the right things."   Photo by Matt Detrich

Jeff Gordon waits to be
introduced to the crowd at
the first NASCAR event at
Chicagoland Speedway,
July 25, 2001.

Photo by Greg Griffo

Gordon has Winston Cup crown all but locked up

Steve Ballard, Friday, October 26, 2001

The key question surrounding Jeff Gordon's pursuit of a fourth Winston Cup championship has changed from if to when.

And where. Mathematically, Gordon could clinch as early as next week's race at Rockingham, N.C. Realistically, he should wrap it up the following week at Homestead, Fla., with two races still to run.

Even Gordon, who has been saying for weeks that the title is up for grabs, is beginning to accept the inevitable. He escaped the danger zones of Martinsville, Va., and Talladega, Ala., unscathed. And he has been down this road enough times—winning in 1995, '96 and '98—to know a 395-point cushion at this stage of the season is virtually unbeatable.

That doesn't mean Gordon is busy polishing his acceptance speech. He goes into the Checker Auto Parts 500 on Sunday intent on winning—especially since Phoenix International Raceway is the only current Winston Cup track on which he has competed five or more times and not won.

"This team really wants to win a Cup race here," said Gordon, who needs to average finishes of 18th or better the rest of the way to lock out closest challenger Ricky Rudd.

"We're not worried about finishing in a certain position during these last few races to guarantee the championship."

Gordon began to take charge the week before the Brickyard 400 and has been in complete control since leaving Indianapolis in early August.

Gordon and Dale Jarrett arrived at Pocono, Pa., tied for the lead with Rudd 28 points behind. By the following week, after Gordon's third victory at Indianapolis Motor Speedway, he was 160 points ahead of Jarrett and 179 ahead of Rudd.

> "That's why this team is where it is and that's why we've won so many races and championships in the past, just because of how strong of a unit they are. And that's why we're going to win races in the future."
>
> —Jeff Gordon

135

Race fans from Des Moines, Iowa, all wearing a familiar rainbow-colored jersey, stand and applaud the announcing of Brickyard pole position holder Jeff Gordon during prerace ceremonies. Jennifer Rowley and Derek Nordhagen lead the group in cheers.

Photo by Mpozi Mshale Tolbert

Gordon has won twice since while posting an average finish of 7.9 in the past 12 races. Rudd has averaged 16.7 and Jarrett 20.0 in that same span, allowing Tony Stewart and Sterling Marlin to chase them down.

Gordon could sit out the next two races and watch Rudd win and still have the lead. But he won't give his pursuers a chance.

"If we can't win, we want to finish as high as possible," Gordon said. "We're not going to change our game plan this late in the season."

Earnhardt
charts course

Dale Earnhardt Jr. handles with aplomb the inevitable comparisons to his late father and even offers a few of his own. So he doesn't figure to be the least bit intimidated when he takes the No. 3 back onto the track for a Busch Grand National race next February at Daytona (Fla.) International Speedway.

Jeff Gordon rides behind Dave Blaney during the early laps of the 2001 Brickyard 400 at Indianapolis Motor Speedway.

Photo by Chris Preovolos

"There is so much that goes into the whole series and into getting these race cars around the track. Your mind is on it so much, whether it be testing or preparing for the race or once you get there for that race weekend and you're in the car. When you're in that car your mind definitely is on nothing else but how can I get this car around the racetrack faster and faster and faster. I guess in a lot of ways it is the place I feel most comfortable, the place that when I get into that car I feel like there's nothing else that's coming into my mind but driving that race car."
—Jeff Gordon

Jeff Gordon prepares himself before the Pepsi 400 at Daytona, July 2001.

Photo Greg Griffo

Earnhardt was becoming his own man before his father was killed in February at Daytona and is more so now. He said he makes decisions on and off the racetrack based on what's right for him and doesn't drive himself crazy trying to figure out what his dad might have said or done.

"I don't put that much pressure on myself," he said. "Every time I make a decision, it doesn't have to be OK with my father."

That doesn't mean he can't use his dad as inspiration. After notching his fifth career win last week at Talladega, Ala., Earnhardt recalled as a youth reading racing magazines and books and finding his father all through them.

"I want to be one of the 50 drivers in that next book," he said. "One day when I've got a son, he can look back and see where his daddy finished in 2001."

A large crowd in the garage watches the crew of the DuPont Chevy driven by Jeff Gordon ready the car for practice on Friday afternoon, Aug. 3, 2001.

Photo by Greg Griffo

139

Jeff Gordon runs a few practice laps during the 2002 season.

Jeff Gordon eyes another Winston Cup championship in 2002. The photo was shot in the garage during testing at Daytona in January.

Photo by Rich Miller

The face of NASCAR

Steve Ballard, Sunday, February 10, 2002

Jeff Gordon deftly handles the very public life of racing star, starts to assume leadership role.

The minute he walked in the door, all activity ceased and all eyes turned. People whispered and pointed, not quite sure what to make of this familiar face invading their familiar surroundings.

Suffice to say that Halifax Lanes could not be described as a celebrity hangout. So when Jeff Gordon materialized at the front desk asking for a pair of bowling shoes, the Monday night clientele was agape.

Yes, most knew longtime Pittsboro, Ind., resident Gordon and his NASCAR Winston Cup brethren were in town for preseason testing at Daytona International Speedway. But they hardly expected to run into him at their local bowling establishment, wandering the racks in search of a ball not too badly chipped with finger holes at least close to the right size.

Once the initial surprise wore off, the line formed quickly. Many people phoned friends or relatives, so the line only seemed to grow.

For most, a quick autograph was enough. They came bearing everything from photographs to scraps of paper to hats to a pair of bowling shoes painted in the DuPont colors of Gordon's sponsor, with a No. 24 on the side.

Some had a story to share or a question to ask while Gordon was signing their offering. Several either brought a camera or raced home to get one. One woman even handed Gordon a cell phone and implored, "Please tell her it's really you."

Between his turns on the lane, Gordon politely handled each and every request. He spent extra time with the kids, especially one with an obvious disability. He smiled through it all and for the most part seemed to be enjoying himself.

"I'm doing good, you know? I'm just really into the team and living my life one day at a time. Things have been going well on the racetrack—I mean, a little up and down, but I've got a lot of people—family and friends—that have been great. They've been there for me, supporting me, and I'm happy."

—Jeff Gordon

NASCAR's brightest star, Jeff Gordon, enjoys some leisure time away from the racetrack at a local bowling alley in Daytona Beach, Fla., after a day of testing in January 2002. Here, Jeff signs autographs for fans between frames. When Gordon entered the bowling alley, unannounced, it was like Elvis Presley had arrived. Nearly everyone in attendance that evening came to ask for an autograph. Gordon graciously signed for everyone who asked.

Photo by Rich Miller

And even if he wasn't, he has accepted better than most modern athletes and entertainers that those people infringing on his time are the very fans who have made him a multimillionaire at age 30. They are the ones who pack speedways around the country 36 times a year, who have pushed NASCAR's TV ratings to record highs and who buy all those T-shirts and caps and model cars.

Gordon said his presence causes less of a stir when he and wife Brooke go to the mall or a movie or bowling alley near their new South Florida home, but privacy is a distant memory.

"You know whenever you're out that somebody is going to come up and tell you they're a fan," Gordon said after posing for a photograph with two local police officers. "They're a big part of this sport. I'm just going to enjoy it while it lasts."

In the
Spotlight

Gordon's ascent to the top of his profession coincides with NASCAR's rapid rise in popularity, leaving few places the four-time Winston Cup champion can go and not be recognized.

The spotlight followed him on trips to Hawaii, Bermuda and London. All are teeming with American tourists, but even the locals recognize the face that has been on so many TV commercials and magazine covers.

In Hawaii, where the nickname of the university's athletic teams is the Rainbow Warriors— same as Gordon's pit crew—he was surprised to go into a bar and be greeted with, "Hey, Jeff Gordon, No. 24."

Bowling, which Gordon took up a few years ago, isn't an ideal way to escape the masses. But his other hobby is, although he views scuba diving more as a way of getting closer to himself.

"It's very relaxing, like going into outer space without having to strap yourself to a rocket," he said. "The deep, slow breaths—it's like yoga. It's just so peaceful."

Perhaps Gordon is more willing to accept the adulation now coming his way after so many years of being booed. Every race and every championship he won came at the expense of Dale Earnhardt or Rusty Wallace or Bill Elliott or any of a dozen other longtime favorites. Gordon was viewed as an interloper who hadn't paid his dues.

Jeff finds bowling, which he took up a couple of years ago, a relaxing hobby.

Photo by Rich Miller

145

Jeff Gordon poses with young fans Taylor Bogard and Rusty Lindenbaum at Atlanta Motor Speedway on March 9, 2002. Gordon also graciously signed autographs for the boys.

Photo by Lynnette Bogard

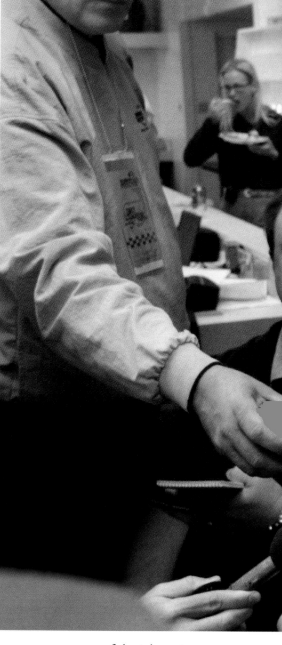

Or perhaps Gordon accepts it as Richard Petty always did—as a necessary part of the job, so it might as well be done right.

Gordon protege Jimmie Johnson, a Winston Cup rookie this season in a car co-owned by Gordon and Rick Hendrick, said most of the advice he has received from Gordon has been about how to handle himself away from the racetrack.

"The first meeting we had, I expected it to be about the nuts and bolts of racing, and it turned out to be about handling my personal life—dealing with the media, with sponsors, with fans and how

to schedule my time to do all that," Johnson said. "He told me to take a day whenever I can for myself, to do nothing. He said to make sure that I keep things balanced."

Gordon probably has more things to balance than any driver in the sport yet does it with apparent ease. He has that unique ability to compartmentalize and prioritize, so though he's always moving he seldom seems hurried.

That at least partially explains why he and Brooke, who recently celebrated their seventh wedding anniversary, have put off starting a family. Fatherhood, in his mind, can't be a part-time job.

Jeff Gordon answers questions from members of the media during a break from testing at Daytona in January.
Photo by Rich Miller

147

Jeff Gordon has achieved great success at an early age but still needs four more championships to pass Richard Petty and Dale Earnhardt for No.1 of all time.

Photo by Rich Miller

"We'd love to have kids someday, but living the way we do now is pretty hectic," he said. "We realize that having a child isn't a take-for-granted type of thing."

In a sport that has just one winner and 42 losers every week, Gordon has learned how not to let his happiness ride on that week's outcome. Win or lose, he puts it behind him and moves on.

"I think everybody wants to be successful," he said, "but you've got to learn to enjoy what you're doing while you're doing it."

That includes bowling, where Gordon reacted to closing out his first game with three consecutive strikes by throwing both arms in the air like he had just won the Daytona 500. He was not about to let the distractions of a reporter and photographer and a horde of fans keep him from having fun.

Still cackling over his prowess, he was summoned by a female fan wanting him to sign the back of her shirt. Afterward, he was asked the strangest thing to which he has been asked to affix his name.

"Body parts," he said with a laugh. "I've had people get me to sign their back or shoulder and then tell me they're going to go get it tattooed. That one blows me away."

NASCAR Spokesman

In the aftermath of Earnhardt's fatal crash last year that left NASCAR grappling with a number of issues, Gordon became more of a spokesman. Four championships and the respect of his peers earned him a place at the podium.

He didn't necessarily relish it but didn't shy away from it, either.

"I've never minded speaking my opinion, but I preferred to do it behind closed doors," he said. "I think last year, with all that happened, a lot of us felt like we needed to be more outspoken. We want to see the sport safe and see it grow. We have a lot invested in it."

Gordon hedges on how many years he has left but has confided in Hendrick—his friend, boss and business partner—that he won't go on indefinitely. Hendrick is hoping for another 10 years, ample time for Gordon to get the four more championships he needs to pass Petty and Earnhardt for No. 1 of all time. Gordon needs 48 wins, or around five a year for 10 years, to pass David Pearson's 105 for No. 2 of all time behind Petty's 200.

"I'd settle for 10 years. By then I'm probably out of it myself," Hendrick said. "That'd make him 40, and I think by then he'll have done everything he wants to do."

What about the 40 or so years he can expect to have left after that? Gordon said he doesn't want to be an owner beyond his partnership with Hendrick but hopes to stay involved in some way. He added, only half-jokingly, that he might start a business that would allow him to indulge his dual pleasures of go-karts and racing video games.

Bowling wouldn't appear to be a career option. He's good enough to hold his own in a beer league but not a candidate for the PBA Tour—unless, of course, the PBA wants to sign him up to draw a crowd.

Driver and car owner Jeff Gordon (left) waits in the garage area at Chicagoland Speedway for practice to begin on July 13, 2002. With him is rookie teammate Jimmie Johnson. Some consider Johnson to be the "next Jeff Gordon."

Photo by Greg Griffo

Jeff Gordon watches his crew work on his car as teams practice at the Indianapolis Motor Speedway on Tuesday, July 30, 2002. Gordon, the defending Brickyard 400 champion, was hoping for a fourth win at the Brickyard 400 on Aug. 4, but it wasn't to be.

Photo by Matt Kryger

Gordon misses out on win No. 4

Michael Pointer, Monday, August 5, 2002

The ultimate 31st birthday present for Jeff Gordon would have been to become the fourth driver to win four races at the Indianapolis Motor Speedway.

But after driving in conditions he called the hottest of his career, the defending Brickyard 400 champ wasn't about to complain about finishing sixth on Sunday—even though it stretched his career-worst streak without a victory to 29 races.

"It was a good birthday," Gordon said. "We're real proud of what we did today, coming from 21st [his starting position] and battling all day long."

The dominating performance by winner Bill Elliott had something to do with that. Elliott's car is owned by Ray Evernham, Gordon's former crew chief at Hendrick Motorsports.

"I couldn't be more happy for those guys," said Gordon, who finished his 52nd consecutive race, one short of Dale Earnhardt's modern-era NASCAR record. "They certainly deserve it. They wore us out today. There was no one in their class."

Gordon won three of the first eight Brickyards and was trying to join open-wheel legends A. J. Foyt, Rick Mears and Al Unser as the only four-time winners at the Speedway.

He never led on Sunday, but there were times he looked like he had a chance to take a place in Speedway history. Gordon had closed to fifth place just 30 laps into the race.

"Well, wins are wins and when you're not winning, you're not winning."
—Jeff Gordon

153

Jeff Gordon goes through his last pit stop before finishing sixth at the 2002 Brickyard 400 at the Indianapolis Motor Speedway.

Photo by Karen Ducey

"I knew we had a good car yesterday in the final practice, but I didn't know we were going to be that good," he said. "I think a lot of guys missed their setups at the beginning of the race because of the heat and ours was just awesome."

After dropping to 26th, Gordon rallied and trailed only Elliott with 50 laps left.

But he couldn't stay consistently close all day and eventually fell back to 11th before rallying for sixth.

A broken oil gauge didn't help. Plus, Gordon said his tires weren't quite as good as he would have liked.

"Unfortunately, we lost the handle on a couple sets of tires and toward the middle of the race, we were fading," he said. "But we kind of regrouped, had some smart calls, came back in and got four tires and got that car going back to the front."

Gordon knows about intense Midwest heat, having graduated from Tri-West High School.

But Sunday's humidity with temperatures in the 90s made conditions almost intolerable.

"Indianapolis is not a real demanding track with it being as flat and big as it is," he said. "But it was just so miserable hot. Thank goodness for the cautions. They allowed all of us to cool down and get some fluids in us and not get dehydrated."

Another consolation: Gordon passed longtime rival and fellow Hoosier Tony Stewart in the final four-lap shootout.

"It's fun setting guys up, especially when the car's right," Gordon said. "You have to take advantage of any opportunity you can, especially when those guys are side by side at the end of the race."

Gordon earned 150 points in the Winston Cup standings. He still is in fourth place, but he shaved 63 points off his deficit and trails leader Sterling Marlin by 125.

"We're real happy with the way things turned out," he said. "Obviously, we wanted to win. But there was only really one car out there that was fast enough to win and that was Bill. If he had fallen out, it would have been a heck of a race."

It was a pretty good day overall for Hendrick Motorsports, which hasn't been as impressive this season as in others. Jimmie Johnson finished ninth, Terry Labonte was 13th and Joe Nemechek was 20th.

"Jeff looked good in the beginning and worked his way up to the top 10, and from where Jimmie started [37th] to where he finished, he was competitive all day," team owner Rick Hendrick said. "We'll just take it and go on."

Added Johnson: "Chad [crew chief Chad Knaus] did an incredible job getting a car that I could drive and our guys on pit road showed up today. They nailed some 13-second stops, got us some great track position, and we were able to hold our own."

> "I'm not trying to create a legacy or anything like that. I'm just trying to live. I think something that's a part of my life is that I have been so blessed and I have been given so many great opportunities in my life that I want to see other people get those opportunities."
> —Jeff Gordon

Jeff Gordon (24) takes the checkered flag to win the NASCAR Sharpie 500 at Bristol Motor Speedway on Saturday, Aug. 24, 2002 in Bristol, Tenn. Jeremy Mayfield is in front of Gordon on the track but trailed in the results.

Photo by Wade Payne

Gordon's Bristol win ends Drought

Jenna Fryer, Sunday, August 25, 2002

Jeff Gordon hoisted the enormous Bristol Motor Speedway trophy over his head, hesitant to ever put it down.

It had been so long since he last stood in victory lane—confetti raining down on him, fireworks popping above—that Gordon wanted to savor every moment of this win.

"It feels like the first one all over again," Gordon said after bumping his way past Rusty Wallace to win the Sharpie 500 on Saturday night and snap his 31-race winless streak.

"I can tell you, we do not take wins for granted. These things are hard to come by and we appreciate them. That moment there in victory lane, I wanted to pause it and burn it into my memory forever because it's just such an awesome, awesome feeling."

For the first 23 races of this season, all Gordon felt was mounting frustration over his inability to get in front and stay there. There were weeks when the Hendrick Motorsports team gave him great cars but driver error sabotaged their efforts.

And there were weeks when the No. 24 Chevrolet was simply junk, unable to even sniff the front of the pack. Races like these left the entire team wondering what had gone so wrong since Gordon wrapped up his fourth Winston Cup championship last November.

For a driver and a team used to dominance—he now has 59 victories in a career that has included 10- and 13-win seasons—not winning since Sept. 30, 2001, was absolute agony.

"When you go as long as we've gone without a win and you realize just how hard it is and how hard you work for them, and just how everything's got to fall in place to get there, you look back and go, 'How in the world did we win 58 races?'" Gordon said.

"It's very flattering to hear comments like that, coming from guys who were my heroes when I was growing up. They left me a lot to live up to."

—Jeff Gordon

Jeff Gordon, front right, hugs team owner Rick Hendrick in victory lane after Gordon won the NASCAR Sharpie 500 on Saturday, Aug. 24, 2002, in Bristol, Tenn.

Photo by Mark Humphrey

Well, he won 47 of them with Ray Evernham as his crew chief and the original "Rainbow Warriors" servicing his cars. But Evernham split midway through the 1999 season to become a car owner, and the Warriors also branched out.

So Gordon had to adjust to new crew chief Robbie Loomis's style and a new crew. It took some time, but they broke through last season with six victories and the Winston Cup title.

Then everything hit a snag, personally and professionally.

He swears he never lost his focus but admits he sometimes wondered what was wrong with him.

"You go through times when you work just as hard and are doing everything the same, and it's just not happening," he said. "You just start to question a lot of things, but not my confidence in my driving. I don't think that I ever really questioned that."

He knew the only thing that could make him happy was a victory, and he wanted that badly.

So Gordon went to Bristol, where he had four career victories but none in the prestigious Saturday night race. He was sure he could get one. He broke a six-race qualifying slump by earning the pole, then led a race-high 235 laps.

But Wallace seemed in control in the waning laps until lapped traffic slowed him and gave Gordon a chance to steal the win. He did it with three laps left in the race, tapping Wallace's Ford enough to knock him out of his way and coast on by.

Jeff Gordon kisses the trophy after winning the NASCAR Sharpie 500 in Bristol, Tenn.
Photo by Mark Humphrey

Wallace, riding a 50-race winless streak, was furious and plotted his revenge. But lapped traffic made it impossible for him to catch Gordon and bump him back.

"I tried desperately to knock the heck out of him; I just couldn't catch him," Wallace said. "It's been a long time since I've won. I guess my day is coming, but, man, I tried real hard."

It was similar to another bump-and-run Gordon put on Wallace to win the spring race at Bristol in 1997. Gordon has no regrets over either episode. With a chance to break his streak, he was going for it.

"If he wants to pay me back, if that's the way he wants to go about it, I've been knocked around, I've been moved out of the way, and I've been wrecked," he said. "I go to the next race, focus on what I've got to do, not taking guys out and doing paybacks.

"He's going to be upset. He lost the race and he wanted it as bad as I did. I don't expect him to be happy. We may talk, we may not talk. We'll just kind of go to Darlington and see what happens. But I'm not calling him."

Celebrate the Heroes of Stock Car Racing
in These Other Acclaimed Titles from Sports Publishing!

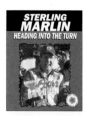

Sterling Marlin:
Heading into the Turn
by Larry Woody
- 5.5 x 7 softcover • 96 pages • photos throughout
- $4.95
- **2002 release!**

Sterling Marlin:
The Silver Bullet
by Larry Woody
- 10 x 10 hardcover • 128 pages • 100 color photos
- $29.95 • Includes cdracecard CD-ROM!
- **2002 release!**

Tony Stewart:
High Octane in the Fast Lane
- 10 x 10 hardcover • 160 pages • color photos
- Includes 60-minute audio CD
- $39.95
- **2002 release!**

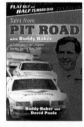

Flat Out and Half Turned Over:
Tales from Pit Road with Buddy Baker
by Buddy Baker with David Poole
- 5.5 x 8.25 hardcover • 200 pages • photos throughout
- $19.95
- **2002 release!**

As They Head for the Checkers:
Fantastic Finishes, Memorable Milestones and Heroes Remembered from the World of Racing
by Kathy Persinger and Mark Garrow (audio)
- 8.5 x 11 hardcover • 160 pages • clr & b/w photos
- Includes audio CD • $39.95 • **2002 release!**

The History of America's Greatest Stock Car Tracks:
From Daytona to the Brickyard
by Kathy Persinger
- Race track shaped h/c • 160 pages • color and b/w photos throughout • $29.95 • **2002 release!**

Dale Earnhardt:
The Pass in the Grass and Other Incredible Moments from Racing's Greatest Legend
by *The Charlotte Observer* and Mark Garrow (audio)
- 10.5 x 10.5 hardcover • 160 pages • color and b/w photos • Includes audio CD • $39.95

StockcarToons:
Grins and Spins on the Winston Cup Circuit
by Mike Smith, cartoonist for the *Las Vegas Sun*
- 11 x 8.5 softcover • 160 pages
- cartoons throughout • $12.95

Dale Earnhardt:
Rear View Mirror
by *The Charlotte Observer*
- 8.5 x 11 hardcover and softcover • 209 pages
- 160+ color and b/w photos throughout
- $29.95 (**hardcover**) • $22.95 (**softcover**)

Dale Earnhardt:
Rear View Mirror (leatherbound edition)
by *The Charlotte Observer*
- 8 1/2 x 11 leatherbound • 209 pages
- 160+ color and b/w photos • $49.95
- **Limited to 1,000 copies!**

Richard Petty:
The Cars of the King
by Tim Bongard and Bill Coulter
- 8.5 x 11 hardcover and softcover • 259 pages
- 500+ color and b/w photos throughout
- $34.95 (**hardcover**) • $24.95 (**softcover**)

Richard Petty:
The Cars of the King (leatherbound edition)
by Tim Bongard and Bill Coulter
- 8.5 x 11 leatherbound • 259 pages • 500+ color and b/w photos throughout • $99.95
- **All copies signed by Richard Petty!**